The **Gardener's Guide** to **STARTING SEEDS INDOORS**

Discover How to Sow, Germinate & Transplant
All the *Veggies*, *Herbs*, *Flowers* & *Fruits*
You **Love** Most

For **Self-Sufficient** Backyard Homesteaders

ELIZABETH GROVE

THE GARDENER'S GUIDE TO STARTING SEEDS INDOORS FOR SELF-SUFFICIENT BACKYARD HOMESTEADERS

DISCOVER HOW TO SOW, GERMINATE, & TRANSPLANT ALL THE VEGGIES, HERBS, FLOWERS, & FRUITS YOU LOVE MOST

ELIZABETH GROVE

"The detail and information given is beyond what I ever expected. So many questions I never asked or thought about were answered. I don't understand how the author could possibly cover everything, but yes, answers are there for any question you have."

- Verified Purchaser

"This was a little gem of a gardening book. I found it to be well formatted, easy to read, well organized, and it provided a ton of information on seed starting."

- Verified Purchaser

"I enjoyed reading this book. I learned more about starting seeds indoors. I wish I had this book at the beginning of the year. I did have some successful seeds that germinated, grew to seedlings and got transplanted into my outdoor garden. There are some helpful tips that I will try next season."

- Verified Purchaser

"it is good, clear, has short sentences, and avoids being convoluted."

- Verified Purchaser

Here's The Plan

INTRODUCTION

CONCLUSION

MY GARDEN CALENDAR

SCAN ME

Use this **tool & spreadsheet** to discover **your zone** and the **best time of year to sow, plant and harvest your fruits & veggies!**

Go to:

WWW.BACKYARDHOMESTEADCOMMUNITY.COM

INTRODUCTION

Disappointments. Wasted time and effort. "Maybe we'll try again next year..."

All things nobody wants to endure after a long season of hope and hard work in the garden. But what if I told you you can be a successful, self-sufficient gardener and that it all starts with **the seed**?

Nothing tastes better than fresh vegetables straight from your own garden, and there's no better feeling than the satisfaction of having a hand in its creation. Self-sufficiency is addicting. The more you do it, the more it becomes a natural way of life. And when you're first starting on the journey, it's not always easy. So, thank you to all the gardeners of the past for making the mistakes that led to a not-so-glorious garden. Me included. Without those disappointments, we wouldn't have all the knowledge and resources to grow our own prosperous, self-sufficient gardens today!

This book will guide you through the entire process of starting seeds indoors and transplanting them outdoors when they're ready. Our past generations have tried and tested the methods used that are guaranteed to work if you follow instructions properly...unlike my first seed starting experience.

When I first introduced myself to gardening, I pictured a backyard homestead with a vast expanse of rich topsoil filled with sprouts, vines, leaves, blossoms, and a lot of promise. I saw rows upon rows of small mounds and those cute, little white garden stakes that are carefully labeled with the vegetable that's supposed to grow. Did you see what I said there? The vegetable that's supposed to grow. My first attempt at creating a backyard garden didn't match my vision of what a garden looked like at all. I lived in a small house with an even smaller yard. I didn't have a vast expanse of rich topsoil, and I definitely didn't have the room to make that happen. But I wanted a garden! And not just any garden, I wanted to try growing my own pumpkins. I loved fall and had always bought lots of pumpkins to carve for Halloween. But they were getting pretty expensive, and it seemed to take me forever to choose "just the right ones" so I thought, why not try growing my own? Most people new to gardening would start with something simple, like radishes or onions. But not me! I had the attitude of "go big or go home" so, without a lot of free space available, I had to get creative.

With an overwhelming selection of seeds and seed starter kits and no prior knowledge of what to choose or why to choose them, I spent what seemed like hours in the gardening section. Eventually, I chose three different packets of pumpkin seeds—Casper pumpkins (have you ever seen a white pumpkin? Yeah, I didn't either that year, but more on that later), small sugar pumpkins, and good 'ol regular jack-o'-lanterns. I bought a basic seed-starter kit that came with a domed tray and had little pods that were already filled with soil. It seemed like it was going to be so easy. It seemed like it would be so easy. Just plant the seeds, water them, and they'd be good to go!

So I followed the instructions on the seed packet (mostly). Sure enough, it didn't take long before I saw the sprouts of baby pumpkin plants! I was so excited; I checked in on my babies multiple times per day. They continued growing day after day, and after just a few weeks, it was time to transplant them outside. I did my research and learned they should be spaced five feet apart and would need at least ten feet to crawl. Wait, what?! Ten feet per plant? I had twelve pods of pumpkins that each had two to three plants started! Remember when I said I followed the instructions (mostly)? Yeah, I added an extra seed to each pod just in case some didn't take. Who knew they all would?! Future note to self: always follow the instructions on the seed packet.

My neighbor saw my struggle and told me I'd have to choose the heartiest ones and pull the rest. This was devastating to me. These were my pride and joy, my labor of love. I couldn't just simply pick the strongest ones and kill off the rest! What was I going to do?

Long story short, I had pumpkin vines growing everywhere. Some in the ground, some in a raised garden bed, a lot of them in five-gallon pails and I also turned one of those small, plastic kiddie pools into a mini garden by drilling holes in the bottom, filling it with soil and six of my pumpkin plants. I know what you're thinking; that doesn't sound like they're five feet apart. You're right. They weren't. I simply didn't have enough space to spread them out to what they needed. So I bought a trellis for them to grow up the wall of my garage, I had vines crawling across the driveway, deeming the driveway unusable and I even had them growing along my fence. I tried anything to give them the room I thought they needed. Guess how many pumpkins I had at the end of the season? Two. After all my love and nurturing to give those guys the best life, I ended up with just two pumpkins.

But you know what? All the hard work and effort was worth it. Those two pumpkins turned out to be the best-looking pumpkins I had ever seen. I had a small sugar pumpkin and a medium-sized jack-o'-lantern. Sadly, none of the casper pumpkins grew that year. But after everything I learned, I tried again the following year with a lot fewer pumpkin seeds and ended up with five beautiful full-grown pumpkins, including two gorgeous casper ones.

Now, five years later, I took what I learned from those darling little pumpkins and expanded my backyard homestead to include everything from lettuce and onions to tomatoes, potatoes, and sugar snap peas. I can't wait to choose what I'm going to plant this year!

The moral of my story is if you've ever dabbled in gardening, you'll know what I mean when I tell you it naturally comes with a lot of trial and error. In my example, I learned as I went. I questioned everything. Did I use the right pods? Do the seedlings have enough sun? Should they be in direct sun? Are they too wet? Did I let them dry up? Should I leave the lid on or off? These are all perfectly normal questions. In fact, they're important to ask so that you have the best chance at producing an excellent yield! Whatever vegetable you want to dabble in, from onions to radishes, pumpkins to corn, each experience is completely unique and comes with an exciting satisfaction that starts as soon as you sow your first seed. I'm here to walk you through with my fool-proof method on how to start seeds indoors.

There is truly nothing more satisfying than growing your own food. I love the idea of living a more self-sufficient lifestyle. And I really love helping people by sharing my story. How I started my passion for gardening, all my pain points and weaknesses, what works and what doesn't! Educating others gives me a greater sense of purpose in my life. I love sharing ideas that some people don't even think about, like when you start your garden from seed instead of buying plants that are already started, you're saving more money and your cost of living diminishes. As you read on, you'll quickly see that everything you're about to learn in this book has come from experience. My step-by-step plan has allowed me to grow and eat all my own vegetables year after year. I'm honestly quite proud of myself for becoming more self-sufficient, and I'm looking forward to getting you excited too. All you need is a little patience, some proper knowledge to get you started, and a whole lot of love.

Throughout my book, you'll learn plenty of tips and tricks to help get you going on starting seeds indoors. You will learn all the best methods for success, how to become more self-sufficient, and you will develop the ability to save money while gardening. When I first started my journey to becoming self-sufficient, I didn't have a clue where to start. I didn't have a "how-to" guide, so I picked up bits and pieces of scattered information from online articles, blog posts, and my grandmother's wisdom. I've taken everything I learned and organized it all in one place to save you the hassle that I went through. It will lead you in the right direction for success, so if you're ready to plant, let's sow!

THE EASIEST SEEDS TO START INDOORS

& THE WORST...

I'M GOING TO LET YOU IN ON A LITTLE SECRET—THE KEY TO starting seeds indoors successfully is learning what they need to actually grow! There's even a magic formula that I'm about to share with you!

Seeds are a lot like humans; they need proper nurturing, love, and attention. Without their fundamental needs being met, they simply will not grow. Period. If you're not providing enough water, for example, no matter how much carbon dioxide you breathe on them as you desperately beg on your hands and knees, willing them to grow—they just won't grow. They're missing a vital piece of the magic formula that leads to their success—water!

Throughout this chapter, I'm going to teach you the fundamentals for giving your seeds a successful start. By the way, I was only half kidding about you needing to beg your seeds to grow. Have you ever heard of people talking to their plants? Well, they were on to something. My Grandmother does this alllll the time. She swears that talking to her plants daily has helped them grow. And it really just makes sense. Every time we speak or breathe, we give off carbon dioxide that's essential for plants to thrive. So, whenever we talk to our little gems, we're breathing life right into them.

Fun Fact! Did you know seeds breathe? Ok, not how you and I do. We can't actually see them breathe, but scientists have observed seeds absorbing oxygen and releasing carbon dioxide. They also take moisture from the air to keep themselves ready for germination. It's like finding life that we didn't know existed!

In Case You Didn't Know: Germination—*The growth of a seed into a young plant or seedling (sprout)*

THE 4 INGREDIENTS IN THE MAGIC FORMULA

1) WATER

When I planted my very first batch of pumpkin seeds, I struggled with knowing how much water to give them. I had to throw out the entire batch! After a couple of weeks, they became covered in fuzzy, white mold from over-watering. They had developed a condition called "damping-off" which happens from being over-watered. It causes their stems to collapse and the seedlings to die. Lesson learned. I started a fresh batch of pumpkin seeds, this time paying closer attention to their watering needs. I used a misting spray bottle (which I found gave me better control of how much water I was giving), and I sprayed them once per day. I sprayed enough water for the soil to look moist but not overly wet. If I noticed the soil looking dry throughout the day, I added a few extra spritzes to stop it from drying out. This has worked wonders for me! Within 10 days of planting the seeds, they germinated, and I had rows of little green sprouts! Hello, life!

General Rule of a Green Thumb:
Use a misting spray bottle to prevent
over-watering.

Now, if you're still unsure about the watering process, there's a self-watering seed-starter kit available in stores or online. It's a simple system created to water seeds automatically, taking the guesswork out of how much water to give. But it also takes the fun out of the germination process. Watering plays a huge part in the ongoing nurturing. Trust me when I say you should have a go at watering manually. You'll save money by not having to buy the system, and you'll have greater satisfaction when you see those first little sprouts start popping up.

2) OXYGEN

Most living things need oxygen to survive. **Three things can affect adequate oxygen levels:**

1. When a seed gets planted in proper conditions, water and oxygen are absorbed through the seed coat. For some seeds like beans or okra, the coat is too thick, stifling the seed's ability to take in adequate water and oxygen. They require a process called **Scarification** (a careful nick to pierce the seed's coat).
2. **Over-watering** causes a lack of oxygen to the seed (think of it as drowning and not being able to breathe).
3. **Planting seeds too deep** in the soil causes a lack of oxygen. If a seed is planted too deep, it expels all its energy before it can reach the surface of the soil and ends up dying off.

So how can you help with oxygen levels? Always read the seed packet thoroughly. Each packet comes with pertinent information relating to the seed's successful germination.

The packet should also give you optimal watering requirements, depth of planting, and the favored lighting conditions for that type of seed.

3) LIGHT

Not all seeds need light equally. For germination to happen successfully, most seeds require darkness, which is why they're usually in the soil. But how deep should they be planted? They all have different requirements listed on their packets. The seed packet is like a mini encyclopedia for each seed. When in doubt, read and follow its directions.

Fun Fact! There are some seeds that you barely press into the soil and some that don't get covered at all. Lettuce, savory, and begonias all require light to germinate, so if they get covered in dirt, it blocks the light from reaching them and germination won't happen. But Cucumbers, marigolds, and tomatoes are impartial to lighting conditions so they will germinate with or without exposure to light

I didn't know this when I first planted my lettuce seeds. I had no clue that seed depth made a difference, so I planted them like any other. My lettuce never grew! There were times where I thought sprouts may have started, but they ended up being weeds. It doesn't seem to matter what conditions there are, weeds seem to always grow and can thrive in any and all circumstances!

Fun Fact! A weed is a plant that has mastered every survival skill except for learning how to grow in rows

· · ·

Once germination has occurred, all seedlings need light to thrive.

General Rule of a Green Thumb:
More light is better!

On average, seeds started indoors need 12-18 hours of light every day. However! Don't give them over 18 hours because they need to rejuvenate in the dark just like we do!

Fun Fact! The reason seeds need darkness is so they can feed themselves the starches and sugars that were created through the cycle of photosynthesis during daylight hours.

In Case You Didn't Know: Photosynthesis—the process in which green plants use sunlight to make their food from carbon dioxide and water. "Photosynthesis is necessary for life on Earth. Without it, there would be no green plants, and without green plants, there would be no animals" (Britannica. 2021). Photosynthesis in plants involves a green pigment called chlorophyll that produces oxygen once carbon dioxide is consumed.

Pro tip! In early spring, the sun's rays are still not strong enough to grow strong seedlings. Even in the sunniest windowsills! This is where artificial light comes in handy to give you the best opportunity for successful growth.

If you're not able to provide sufficient lighting for your seedlings naturally, there's a wide range of supplemental lighting available. Fluorescent lights mounted by chains and S-hooks are the easiest solution. Not only are they cheaper than buying special growing lights (remember, we want to be successful while trying to be sustainable and self-sufficient) they're also easy to adjust to accommodate the distance between the lights and the growing seedlings. You want to keep the lights close to the tallest gems and raise the lights as they grow even taller by shortening up the chain using the S-hooks.

General Rule of a Green Thumb:
Seeds like to be warm during the day and cooler at night

4) TEMPERATURE

The most common temperature needed for most seeds started indoors to reach germination is between 70-90°F. If you don't live in a home that stays within this temperature range (I don't know many people who do besides my grandfather, who likes his house as warm as the Sahara desert), then you'll need a source of artificial heat. Place your little gems in sweet-spot areas like the furnace room (which is usually warmer than the rest of the house) near a wood stove or heat register, or use a heated blanket, mat, or pad that lays nicely under your seed containers. Something to keep in mind—this only applies until germination. Once your little gems sprout (germinate), move them to your optimal light source, whether it be natural or artificial.

I'll go into more detail on lighting and temperature in **Chapter 3: Let There Be Light & More.**

Now that you have the 4 magic ingredients for success, let's talk about some of the easiest seeds for beginners to start with! (C. Boeckmann. 2021, January 6) You'll notice I often mention using an organic seed-starting mix. Don't overwhelm yourself with what this means. For now, just consider it as soil and I'll discuss how to choose the ideal starting mix (soil) in **Chapter 2: Soil or Spoil.**

BASIL

I just love the smell of fresh basil! Start your basil seeds indoors 6-8 weeks before the last frost in spring. Sow seeds ¼ inches deep in organic seed-starting soil. Keep the soil moist at 70°F. Seedlings will sprout in 7-14 days.

COLEUS

Year after year, I use Coleus as a filler in my flower garden. They're one of my favorites and are so fun to grow! They turn out so luscious and full! Come fall time, I have a hard time pulling them! They always look so hearty and robust. To grow your own coleus, plant your seeds indoors 6-8 weeks before the last frost using a seed starting kit. Sow seeds so that they're lightly covered with organic seed-starting soil. The finer the better. They germinate best in temperatures between 65-75°F. Sprouts should start in 12-21 days.

KALE

Sow 3-4 seeds ¼" deep in organic seed-starting soil. The optimal soil temperature should be between 50-85°F. Seeds should germinate in 7-10 days. Thin out, leaving the strongest plants before transplanting.

Fun Fact! Kale is a superfood!

In Case You Didn't Know: Superfood—a term used for certain foods that are packed with essential nutrients and said to have a variety of health benefits!

LEAF LETTUCE

This one's super fun to try since it grows fairly quickly, so don't leaf this one out! Seeds should sprout in 7-15 days. Some leaf varieties reach maturity in as little as 30 days, while others require 6-8 weeks to reach full harvest size. Sow seeds ¼" deep, keeping them close to the surface of the soil where the soil should remain evenly moist. The optimal soil temperature ranges between 50-72°F.

MARIGOLDS

Sow indoors 6-8 weeks before the last frost. Cover the seeds with vermiculite (a type of mineral that helps to keep moisture and good aeration) and provide a soil temperature of 70-75°F. Seeds should sprout in 4-14 days.

Pro Tip! Marigolds are easy to grow, which is a good thing because the birds love to eat them! I usually grow a couple of rounds of marigolds so I can replace the ones that the birds have so kindly destroyed! Thank you sparrows and ravens...

MELONS

It's essential to start melon seeds indoors around mid to late April, as they need to be transplanted outside when the plants are just 5 weeks old. Their preferred soil temperature to reach germination is between 68-77°F. You should see sprouts within 5-10 days.

NASTURTIUMS

I'd be willing to bet you pronounced this one wrong—I know I did! Pronounced nə'stərSHəm, the Oxford dictionary defines this beauty as "a South American trailing plant with round leaves and bright orange, yellow or red edible flowers." (Myefe. (2020, December 1). *SW7 Single*.) They're widely grown as ornamental flowers. To try growing your own nasturtiums, sow seeds ¼"-½" deep in organic seed-starter soil. They prefer darkness during germination, followed by bright light once sprouted. The best soil temperature for germination is between 55-65°F. Seeds will sprout in 7-12 days.

BELL PEPPERS

With the choice of red, green, orange, or yellow, which one's your favorite? I like both red and green, but these basic instructions apply to all. Sow pepper seeds only ¼" deep in organic soil. Most seeds sprout in about 7 days at a temperature of 70-80°F. The germination of peppers can vary depending on the variety. Peppers are very sensitive to cold temperatures, so make sure frost is entirely out of the picture before transplanting them outdoors.

Fun Fact! Red peppers are actually green peppers in disguise. Whaaat??! Yup! They just stay on the plant until they're fully matured. In fact, most peppers start out being some shade of green until they've matured or ripened.

SNAPDRAGONS

Best sown on the surface of an organic seed starter mix, these beauties make a marvelous addition to any flower garden. They like to be kept in bright light and to maintain a soil temperature of about 55°F. Seeds should sprout in 10-21 days. Snapdragons are prone to damping off, so increase their ventilation by applying a thin layer of vermiculite on top of the soil and water only from below. The easiest way to do this is by putting water directly in the tray that your flat sits in and let the seeds soak up the moisture from underneath.

SPINACH

Another superfood, and it seems to have the most effortless instructions! Sow seeds ½" deep in organic seed-starter soil and maintain a temperature between 45-70°F. Seeds should sprout in 7-14 days.

CHERRY TOMATOES

Plant seeds about ⅛" deep and press gently on the soil to make sure the seeds have just enough contact with the soil. Keep them in a dark, warm location between 70-80°F. Tomato seeds will usually germinate in 5 to 10 days in optimal conditions. Like peppers, tomatoes are also very sensitive to cold temperatures, so you want to be sure that frost warnings are done for the season before transplanting them outdoors.

Pro Tip! To conserve moisture, cover tomato seeds loosely with plastic wrap.

General Rule of a Green Thumb:
Knowledge is knowing a tomato is a fruit; Wisdom is not putting it in a fruit salad.

There you have it! My compilation of the easiest seeds to start indoors. Because gardening comes with its difficulties and challenges, let's briefly discuss a few of the most challenging seeds to grow to avoid any unnecessary disappointments or hiccups along your beginner's journey.

Starter Seeds

Seed Type	Sow Depth	Soil Temp	Days to Germ
Basil	1/4"	70	7-14
Coleus	1/8"	65-75	12-21
Kale	1/4"	50-85	7-10
Leaf Lettuce	1/4"	50-72	7-15
Marigolds	1/8"	70-75	4-14
Melons	1/2"	68-77	5-10
Nastriums	1/4"-1/2"	55-65	7-12
Bell Peppers	1/4"	70-80	7
Snapdragons	surface	55	10-21
Spinach	1/2"	45-70	7-14
Cherry Tomatoes	1/8"	70-80	5-10

SEEDS NOT RECOMMENDED FOR BEGINNERS

As a beginner, I recommend staying away from plants that either don't transplant well and those that despise being transplanted at all! Yes, plants are just as temperamental as some humans. This is because they hate having their roots disrupted. They enjoy being comfortably nestled inside their pot or pod, but when it comes time to move, they detest it! I mean, who actually enjoys moving anyway?

When I first transplanted my pumpkins, I ended up putting them through transplant shock (the stress a plant endures from being transplanted). They went from having healthy, happy-looking leaves to weak, sad-looking leaves. They looked terrible! And I felt utterly horrible! To make matters worse, I made the same mistake that most amateurs make; I tried compensating by adding more water. And that's a big no-no. When leaves look wilted, you automatically think they must need more water! Not in this case. We'll talk more about the do's and don'ts of transplanting in **Chapter 9: Good Ol' Outdoors.**

Plants that don't transplant well and are best started outdoors are cucumbers, muskmelon, pumpkin, squash, and watermelon. Notice how I mentioned pumpkin? (It's not that they don't like being transplanted, it just seems to take trial and error to get it right). I perfected that process in my second year of trying.

Then there are plants that resist being transplanted at all. Root vegetables like carrots and beets hate having their roots disturbed, so it's best to start these babies outdoors directly in the ground. Plants like dill and parsley have long taproots, so they also despise being transplanted and should be started directly outdoors. There are other factors besides transplanting that pose an issue for beginners: temperature, moisture levels, and soil specifications all contribute to making some seeds a definite deterrent for beginners. I'm not saying you shouldn't try them, I just want to inform you of their risks as I hate the idea of you being disappointed and discouraged if things don't go right due to them being difficult seeds to grow!

Carrots are a root vegetable that requires special care. Its key challenge is its soil preparation. They need at least 6" of loosened soil to do well. Carrots are also finicky on the type of soil you use. They don't like clay soil, but mineral and humus soil work well. You also want to avoid any soil that has pebbles or any form of obstruction as that makes the carrots grow around the blockage. This leads to a funny-looking carrot! If you don't have the right soil available in your main garden, you can grow carrots in raised garden beds where you can control the type of soil.

Fun Fact! The next time you see a carrot that has bumps and lumps and is not-so-straight, you'll know that a pebble or obstruction in the soil caused its warped figure!

Cauliflower, broccoli, and cabbage (who are all from the same family called **brassicas**) have a long growing season and can be temperamental with their temperature preference. They don't like it too hot or too cool, it's got to be just right. Which, depending on where you live, can be hard to maintain. Their ideal temperature ranges between 65-80°F. They're also a bug's delight, which makes them fall victim to cabbage worms and disease.

Fun Fact! I consider a long growing season to be between 120-180 days. If you do the math, that's equivalent to needing a growing season of between 17-25 weeks!

Celery is famous for turning out as all leaves and no stalk. It requires a ton of moisture, so plant celery in soil that allows for maximum water retention. It needs consistent watering and is a burden to some gardeners just for that reason. Celery also has a long growing season and needs cooler temperatures to thrive.

Head Lettuce can be quite the challenge, and it takes a lot of work to get that perfectly shaped head that you see in stores. Unlike leaf lettuce, head lettuce requires uniform watering and consistent temperatures. They don't do well with temperature fluctuations as it causes them to bolt prematurely, and even the slightest contrast between sun and shade can lead to bolting. When lettuce bolts, it has a very unpleasant taste.

. . .

In Case You Didn't Know: Bolting *is a term used when plants attempt to produce seeds and reproduce before it gets harvested. Plants like lettuce, broccoli, basil, cilantro, and cabbage are most susceptible to early bolting. When they prematurely bolt, plants will grow in height very rapidly and then go to seed.*

In this chapter, I touched on the importance of the magical formula for success. **Water, light, oxygen, and temperature are crucial components for successfully growing seeds indoors.** In future chapters, I'll go a little more in-depth on the what's, where's, why's, when's, and how's of each component and how they relate to different seeds. I also gave you a list of my favorite seeds to start indoors that should get you significant results and a list of my not-so-favorites (at least until you're a seasoned pro) to avoid disappointment and discouragement. I hope that you're excited to continue this beautiful journey of self-sustaining backyard homesteading and that you look forward to reaping all of its joyous rewards. It's entirely worth it, I mean it from my head *tomatoes.*

Gardeners know all the Dirt

2

SOIL

OR SPOIL...

When you create an organic, self-sustaining garden that can feed you and your family year-round, you'll notice the food you produce tastes better than anything bought. Lettuce is crispier, beans are heartier, carrots are crunchier, and celery is juicier. Avoiding the use of expensive commercial and synthetic products makes a tremendous impact on the environment and your garden's long-term success. Your crops will be healthier and so will your wallet.

Creating an inexpensive, self-sustaining garden is something I take a lot of pride in. There's nothing more fulfilling than having a garden bed full of DIYs, so if you've been dreaming of creating an inexpensive, self-sustaining garden for yourself, follow these **5 basic steps:**

1. Make organic soil from scratch
2. Water for free using Mother Nature. Hello, rain!
3. Get creative with your pots! Anything from cottage cheese or yogurt containers to milk cartons or disposable aluminum loaf pans makes for great repurposed choices. (Chapter 6: Party Thyme) Or start from scratch and create your own using newspaper

16

4. Make your own fertilizer for a fraction of the cost of store-bought brands **(Chapter 8: It's Kind of a Big Dill)**
5. Harvest and save seeds so you can use them again **(Chapter 10: I Beg Your Garden?)**

Fun Fact! Make little seedling pots by tearing strips of newspaper into roughly 6″ strips, wrap each strip around a small glass or bottle, letting about 2″ of extra paper stick out from the bottom, tuck the extra paper under the glass or bottle, slip the paper pot off the glass and fill it with your starter-mix to keep its shape. You can later transplant these innovative pots, paper and all! What a fun, money-saving idea!

Soil is the foundation for the success of your garden. Good soil promotes lush growth and large yields, while great soil provides that AND is low cost and organic. Double the benefits, double the fun! I've tried several types of soils and mixes, from store-bought to a slew of DIY concoctions. There are so many methods of creating your own soil for seed-starting, but I've found best success in using a DIY seed-starting mix that needs only 3 ingredients. When combined, these simple, organic ingredients provide the ultimate level of drainage, texture, and water retention. (Gary Heilig, Michigan State University Extension. 2021, March 9)

THE 3 MAGIC INGREDIENTS FOR A GREAT ORGANIC SEED-STARTER MIX (SOIL)

1. SPHAGNUM PEAT MOSS

(if you prefer to be as sustainable as possible, avoid peat moss by substituting it for coco-coir or see my list of alternatives below)

One of the most significant advantages of using peat moss in seed-starting is that it's sterile. Being naturally antiseptic, it stops bacteria and fungi from harming your seeds. We already know we don't want our soil too wet, so peat moss (or its alternative) allows for excellent drainage and great aeration. It's fine in texture, making it pleasant to work with and doesn't have many built-in nutrients, meaning you have better control of what's going into your soil.

Fun Fact! Peat moss can absorb 16-26 times its weight in water, so don't be surprised by how much it expands!

There's one huge disadvantage to peat moss, and it was enough for me to switch to one of its alternatives. Some people prefer to stay away from sphagnum peat moss because of how long it takes to replenish. The ecosystems they support are being destroyed, and the peat isn't being replenished as fast as the farmers and gardeners are using it. If we don't at least try to refrain from using peat moss, eventually the ecosystems that the peat bogs support will disappear. I'm all for being as sustainable as possible, so I converted to peat-free and use **coco-coir** as my alternative.

As well as being equal to peat moss in their soil aeration, drainage, and increased water retention, the following alternatives have their own unique benefits.

Coco-coir is like peat moss in the way it looks, feels, and retains water. The difference is in its name. Coco-coir is made from coconut husks, while peat moss is made from layers and layers of organic materials that have been decomposing for thousands of years. Neato! Coco-coir makes a great substitution because it has all the same characteristics as peat moss with the bonus of having a neutral pH. This means it won't add or diminish the acidic level of your soil.

Compost is organic waste from your kitchen, such as eggshells, vegetable peelings, and fruit waste. Compost breaks down and slowly releases its nutrients into your soil mix.

Worm castings (also called vermicast) is essentially worm poo that's full of nutrients and microorganisms

Composted bark has a slow breakdown and prevents plants from being starved of nitrogen

2. PERLITE

What I'm about to tell you may disappoint you. You know those tiny styrofoam balls that you often see mixed in soil? They're not actually styrofoam balls! They're bits of perlite! Perlite is a volcanic material that gets superheated to a point where it pops like popcorn and becomes 13 times its size. Once popped, small air tunnels are created. These air tunnels help to retain the moisture, oxygen, and nutrients that need to get to the roots of your plants. Perlite helps keep your soil fluffy by resisting compaction and promoting good aeration. It has a natural filtration system that makes excess water efficiently drain away while keeping enough moisture and the essential nutrients that are vital to your plants' success.

3. VERMICULITE

In its original form, vermiculite looks a lot like mica. In its horticultural form, it's made using superheat just like perlite. The high heat allows it to expand into pieces shaped like little accordions, resulting in a ton of layers of thin plates. In its horticultural form, vermiculite is everlasting. It's odorless, non-toxic, and sterile, and it won't rot, break down, or mold. It usually has a neutral pH (depending on its source), is light to the touch, and mixes well with other soils. It improves soil aeration, increases moisture retention (even more so than perlite), and readily absorbs essential nutrients like potassium, calcium, and magnesium, which are all necessary for quicker growth! (Gardener's Supply Company. 2021, May 4)

. . .

In Case You Didn't Know: Micas *are a group of minerals whose individual crystals can be split into very thin elastic plates and make some rocks sparkle! Micas are most often found in igneous rocks (like granite), metamorphic rocks (marble), and small flakes can occasionally be found in sedimentary rocks (sandstone or limestone). So pretty!*

Pro Tip! Vermiculite is commonly used in construction, so be sure to choose horticultural vermiculite when doing your shopping. The horticultural version will be free of toxins and additives that could otherwise be dangerous to your seedlings.

In a nutshell, mixing **peat moss** (or its alternative) with **perlite** and **vermiculite** is the magic formula for ultimate success. You'll have the greatest water retention, the best soil aeration, the easiest delivery of essential nutrients, and best of all, it's fun to make! I hope I'm not making it sound like a lot of work to make your seed starting mix from scratch. It's really not. You may be a bit put off by the initial startup investment of having to buy three separate ingredients to make one soil, and you may even be thinking that it would be so much easier to just buy a pre-mixed one. And you're right, it would be! But let me tell you this: the small start-up cost of these 3 ingredients will go a long way towards your self-sustainable, backyard homesteading, gardening journey. Whew, that was a mouthful! You'll get double, if not triple the amount of homemade, organic soil vs. buying a pre-made seed-starting mix. You'll have complete control of and know exactly what's in your mix (and how each ingredient benefits your seedlings), and if you keep your ingredients dry, they'll never go bad! You'll have plenty left over to make your mix over and over again. See why I said making your own goes a long way?

Peat Moss/
Coco Coir

Perlite

Vermiculite

Magic
Seed Starter
Mix

Before I knew I could make my own starter soil, I was buying bags of pre-made soil. Believe me when I say the start-up cost of making your seed-starter mix is well worth it. When I first started making my own mix, I bought the 3 magic ingredients once and still have plenty leftover. I'll often add some to my outdoor garden beds and potting soils to add some freshness and to give better water retention and aeration. And I've yet to run out of soil! No more repeated trips to the store, no more running out, and best of all, no more spending oodles of money on something I can easily make myself. Three cheers for backyard homesteading!

If only I knew then what I know now. But we live and learn, and I'm so excited to be passing all this knowledge on to you. If you've never tried making a seed-starter mix before, now's the time to get your hands dirty!

WHAT YOU'LL NEED TO START YOUR MIX:

- Optional Gardening gloves (I prefer to skip the gloves and use my bare hands. I love connecting with Mother Nature, it's such a grounding experience for me)
- Sterile tub or bucket
- Water for mixing (preferably distilled or rainwater if you've been collecting)
- Equal parts peat moss or its alternative, perlite, and vermiculite (you can choose what your "part" consists of. It can be a scoop, a pail, or an entire bag of each as long as they're added equally)

That's it! The recipe for this magic potion is quite simple:

- Take equal parts peat moss or alternative, perlite, and vermiculite and combine them in your tub or bucket
- Soak the mixture with water
- Now the fun part—stick your hands in and connect with nature as you stir the mixture around. Feel the soil mixing as you squish it between your fingers, letting it fall back into your bucket. You're looking for a moist but not "dripping" texture. Compare it to the sand that you would make sandcastles with. As you do this, take a second to close your eyes and focus on the feel of the soil in your hands. Feel yourself connecting with the earth and welcome its energy as it flows through your fingers to the rest of your body.

Grounding can be a very calming experience. It promotes mindfulness and relaxation. But hey, if you'd rather just get down and dirty without thought, or if you prefer to use a trowel and not get dirty (or as little as possible), that's ok too. I'm just here to guide you through.

In Case You Didn't Know: Grounding is a mindfulness exercise that connects your energy to the earth. It allows you to be more aware of your body and feelings, be in the present moment, and receive revitalizing energy from the earth. By practicing grounding, you'll get more in tune with your mind and body, your talents and gifts, you'll realize your value in the world, and reaching your visions and goals will become easier. It helps to clear out negative energy, paving the way for positive energy to shine through. Grounding has done wonders for me. I've made it a regular practice in my life, especially when I'm spending time in the garden. And you don't have to be full of soil to do it. Just taking a walk outside barefoot, letting your feet touch the ground, or sit against a tree, letting the palms of your hands touch the surrounding earth. You can lie in the sand or go for a swim in the sea. As long as you focus your thoughts on connecting with the earth, you're transferring energy and practicing grounding!

General Rule of a Green Thumb:

If you choose not to make your own seed-starter mix, use soil that's made specifically for growing seedlings. Don't use soil from an existing garden or reuse soil from houseplants. You need to start with a fresh, sterile blend to give your seedlings the best start. Anything old or reused can lead to unhealthy, diseased seedlings. (*Make the Best Seed Starting Mix for Dirt Cheap. 2021, February 6*).

WHAT TO LOOK FOR IN PRE-MADE SOIL MIXES:

- Lightweight

- Grainy texture
- Mentions good water retention on the packaging
- Lists sphagnum peat moss, coco coir, perlite, and/or vermiculite as key ingredients

Were you surprised to learn that my seed-starting mix doesn't contain any actual soil? A good organic seed-starting mix needs ingredients with excellent drainage capabilities and good moisture, oxygen, and nutrient retention. That's all your seeds look for in a good starter mix to germinate and promote strong, healthy roots. The actual soil ingredient gets added later when making a potting mix for your seedlings to be transplanted outdoors in. For now, equal parts of each of the magic ingredients, sphagnum peat moss (or its alternative), perlite, and vermiculite make up the magic potion that's needed for your seeds to get a good head-start on becoming healthy seedlings. Since you know exactly what's in your seed-starting and you've watched your seedlings grow successfully in it, you can reuse the mix as long as your seedlings were disease and insect-free. Just reuse it once, though! After using it for a second season, you can dump the mix in your garden and start a fresh batch in the spring. If you choose to reuse your starter mix for the next season, be sure to let it dry completely before packing it away for the winter.

Thank you for reading!

Enjoying so far?

Scan the QR code below
to leave a review!

3

LET THERE BE LIGHT

& MORE

WELCOME TO CHAPTER 3! UP TO THIS POINT, I'VE BRIEFLY TALKED about the essential equipment needed for successful indoor seed-starting. Throughout this chapter, I'm going to follow up on those basics by going into greater detail on how and why each piece of equipment is vital to your success.

SEED CONTAINERS AND TRAYS (POTS)

Ok, so earlier I talked about being thrifty by reusing some everyday household objects to use as containers. I even gave you a fun DIY project for making newspaper pots. But I also have two container methods that I've had outstanding success with as well.

CONTAINER METHOD #1: THE 6-CELL 1020 SEED-STARTING SYSTEM

These six-cell packs are made from durable recycled polypropylene plastic that'll last for years to come. They look a lot like the flimsy six-packs that you buy your plants or flowers in from the garden center, with a few improvements.

- There's a large hole in the bottom of each cell, big enough to stick your finger in to push your seedling out with ease when it's time for transplanting. The large hole also aids in root development, stops the roots from tightly swirling up at the bottom of its container, and allows for easy bottom watering
- There are spaces at each of the four corners that stay open to promote the oxygen that seeds need
- They are super-strong and will last for years to come. I've seen people stand on them!

The trays that these containers sit in are called **propagation trays**. There's a standard size available referred to as "1020". It's 1" in height and will hold 12 of the polypropylene six-packs. That's 72 seedlings! Using the six-pack system allows for greater flexibility in managing your seedlings. Not all seeds germinate and grow at the same pace, so being able to handle just the seeds that are ready for trans-planting makes the process a heck of a lot easier to manage. Using the standard size tray allows you to use the standard size humidity domes, which are made to fit the 1020s perfectly. (*Epic Gardening. 2021, February 15*)

CONTAINER METHOD #2: THE 24-CELL SEED-STARTING TRAY

These cells are larger than the 6-pack setup but are just as durable. It's matched with a tray and a platform that sits in the tray to hold a capillary mat. Water is added to the tray, the platform is set inside the tray, and the mat sits on top of the platform. One end of the mat extends down into the water, which wicks the water up to soak the mat. The seedling tray is set atop the mat and is then bottom fed with the water from the mat. There's a humidity dome that fits over the tray and completes the seed-starting system. I use this system when I sow all the same seeds, or at the very least, all my seeds that have the same germination and growing needs. Otherwise, it becomes quite cumbersome to move the entire 24-pack tray to transplant just a few seedlings. (*Epic Gardening*. 2019, *March 3*)

If you're interested in learning more about the specific seed-starting trays that I like to use, feel free to email me at:

contact@backyardhomesteadcommunity.com

By now, you should have a good idea of how to choose and use containers and trays. Now you'll learn more about how a seed is just a miracle waiting to happen. And all it takes is the right environmental conditions.

Fun Fact! Your seeds are alive! They just remain in an inactive state (dormant) before being planted. They still take in oxygen, give off carbon dioxide and slowly use up all the stored food that's naturally built inside of them.

Seeds in their original form are already living. They have an embryo that's able to germinate and produce a new plant. They also have individual needs and preferences such as optimal temperature, humidity, and moisture levels. Seeds, like every living thing, have a circle of life. They germinate, grow into seedlings, and then turn into full-grown plants. At the end of the growing season, their cycle is usually over. But their seeds can be harvested and saved so the process can be reproduced again next year!

Dormant seeds are constantly monitoring their external environment. Each type of seed waits for its ideal environmental conditions before it breaks its dormancy and becomes active by germinating. The seedlings go through photosynthesis for energy and depend on the soil for adequate nutrients and moisture, which is absorbed through its roots. Your job is to provide all the proper external environmental factors that your seeds need to survive and thrive.

Most seeds prefer their soil to be kept at a temperature range of between 68-86°F. Always read the packet to know for sure that your particular seeds fall into this range. The closer the seeds are to having their ideal soil temperature, the quicker germination will happen.

Pro Tip! Once germination occurs, the best temperature for growing your little seedlings is about 10° cooler than the temperature needed to get to germination.

---

*In Case You Didn't Know: The ideal temperature that seeds need is based on the temp of the soil, not air temperature. Sure, having a nice warm house will help but be sure to monitor soil temp too. This can easily be done using a soil thermometer or gauge. A **soil thermometer** is just a regular thermometer attached to a long metal probe that gets poked into the soil about 1-3" deep. This depth will give you the most accurate reading.*

Frugal Tip! A meat thermometer from your kitchen will also do the trick!

Humidity (not to get mixed up with temperature) is just as important for germination. Seeds like to be kept moist, not soaked, and soggy. They need to take in oxygen but don't be too careful with your watering or the soil may dry out, causing your seeds to die.

I didn't mean to scare you! I'm sorry! I know how overwhelming this process can be. But if you follow my lead, you'll be fine.

THE MAGIC HUMIDITY FORMULA

1. Sow your seeds according to the depth on the packaging
2. Gently mist the soil with your handy spray bottle. When the soil has darkened and appears wet, that's usually a sign to stop spritzing
3. Keep the humidity in by covering the tray with plastic (you can use plastic wrap, bags, or a humidity dome)
4. As soon as you see sprouts, germination has occurred and the covering should be removed
5. Check your seedlings twice per day for moisture. You can tell how wet they are by the color of the soil
6. Let the soil surface dry between waterings

OPTIONAL EQUIPMENT: HUMIDIFIERS

If you need some help regulating the humidity in your seed-prepping area, there are a variety of humidifiers that can be used depending on your setup. To help you better understand what you may need, here are the 3 basic humidifiers:

Ultrasonic Humidifier: This one's known as the best option for starting seeds indoors because of its versatility and ease of use. In addition to controlling humidity, it can be set to give both warm and cool mist, allowing for better temperature control of your growing area.

Cool Mist Humidifier: Just as the name says, this type of humidifier produces cool, invisible moisture. It increases humidity and removes heat from the air. A cool-mist humidifier uses less energy and can be run for a longer period of time vs. a warm-mist humidifier.

Warm Mist Humidifier: The most common type on the market. When your room is a little too cool for your seeds' liking, a warm mist humidifier can raise the temperature of the room slightly while adding moisture to the air.

Pro Tip! How do you know if you need a humidifier? If you find the area where you keep your little gems has trouble staying warm (at its optimal temp), you may want to consider using a warm mist humidifier. If the area is too warm already, try using a cool-mist humidifier. Either way, the added moisture benefits most seeds, and as a bonus, it benefits people and furniture too! Keep in mind that seeds need proper air circulation to ward off disease despite their love of humidity.

OPTIONAL EQUIPMENT: OSCILLATING FANS

Using a fan is a trick that my grandmother taught me. We were sitting outside together in her bountiful garden, full of all the delicious veggies you can imagine. As I sipped my tea, I told her about losing my first batch of leaf lettuce. I described the symptoms: skinny stems, stunted roots, white cobweb growth on the roots and top of the soil. She explained this condition as a disease called **damping off**, which is caused by fungus or mold that grows when there's too much moisture present. She sensed my disappointment and suggested I set up a fan or two and try my lettuce again. I did exactly as she said, and a few weeks later I had some healthy lettuce sprouts! Thanks, grandma!

. . .

One way to prevent your seedlings from diseases like damping-off is to keep a fan nearby, letting it run 24/7. This ensures continuous air movement, which helps keep the surface of the soil dry. You don't want the breeze too strong though, the seedlings won't like that. Keep it at a low setting and don't keep the fan pointed directly at your little gems. Oscillating on low is fine. Along with preventing disease, a fan will help to get your seedlings used to having some "wind gusts" and helps with the hardening off process, which will be discussed later in **Chapter 8: It's Kind of a Big Dill.** When seedlings get accustomed to flowing in the breeze, they seem happier as they develop heartier stems and stand taller and firmer. (*Germinating Seeds Indoors & Caring for Seedlings. 2018, March 9*)

LIGHTING

LED or fluorescent lights are best to use for starting seeds indoors. Grow lights provide color options for each stage of seedling growth. They're so easy to use and have a quick setup. Being low wattage, the bulbs are cool to the touch, energy-efficient, and last a long time. Grow lights come in so many shapes, sizes, and configurations that only you can decide what's best for your particular setup. I'm sure as I explain a little about each type of light, you should be able to narrow down your options, hopefully making it easier to choose. (*Lighting options for starting seed (LEDs vs. Fluorescent). 2020, March 2*)

Freestanding Units:

- Has one or two tiers for plant trays
- Comes in fixed sizes and needs space to accommodate
- Available with LED or fluorescent bulbs
- Some include casters for easy movement

Cart Units:

- Usually has one or two tiers
- Freestanding with castors
- A smaller option than most freestanding units

Stackable Modular Units:

- Similar to freestanding units but allows for expansion if you later decide to add to your indoor garden space

Countertop Models:

- **Compact -** Ideal for small spaces and small indoor gardens
- **Mini Greenhouse Domes -** A complete system designed for tabletop seed germination
- **Hydroponic Grow Systems -** Compact kits include everything needed to grow all your favorite kitchen herbs without soil

(*13 of the Best Grow Lights for Indoor Plants and Seedlings. 2021, March 22*)

DIY Light System:

Let's not forget about the classic DIY lighting system that I talked about in **Chapter 1: The Easiest Seeds to Start Indoors.** Available in many fixture lengths (depending on your setup) Mount your light fixture using chains and S-hooks to easily accommodate all stages of growth

.   .   .

If you'd like more information on the specific lighting equipment I've had great success with, please email me at:

Contact@backyardhomesteadcommunity.com

OPTIONAL EQUIPMENT: TIMERS

The convenience of a timer ensures your seedlings have sufficient light exposure without you having to worry about it. Simply set your timer to run for 12-16 hours during the day. Your little gems already depend on you so much for everything, do yourself the favor and invest in an inexpensive timer to do the lighting work for you and avoid forgetting this crucial step! I found that having a timer was a fantastic investment, as I was often guilty of forgetting to turn the lights on, especially on those bright, sunny days. Thank you, timer!

OPTIONAL EQUIPMENT: HEATING MATS AND HUMIDITY DOMES

Heating mats are used to maintain the desired temperature of the soil for germination. Once germination has occurred, the mat is no longer needed and should be immediately removed. Only select seeds seem to need the mat. Peppers and tomatoes like the heat mat as long as you take it away as soon as they sprout. Nobody likes hot soil. Broccoli, cabbage, and lettuce don't like the heat mat at all because they prefer their soil to be kept cooler.

Humidity domes are used to keep the moisture in until seeds germinate. Once you spot some sprouts, it's time to remove the dome.

. . .

Using both mats and domes together can be dangerous to the growth of your seeds. Seeds need heat to germinate, but heat mixed with humidity can lead to mold and mildew and cause damping off. Mold spores, mildew, and bacteria thrive in really warm environments, so knowing this, I prefer to avoid using a mat and dome together. Instead, I usually go with whichever one is best for the needs of my seeds.

General Rule of a Green Thumb:

ALWAYS turn off the heating mat or remove the dome as soon as your seeds start to sprout. **When in doubt, watch for sprout!**

In this chapter, I introduced a couple of seed-starting systems—**the 6-cell 1020 system and the 24-cell system.** For small-time gardeners or those new to being backyard homesteaders, the 6-cell 1020 system seems to be the more convenient method. But it also holds true everybody has their preferences so by all means, experiment to see which one becomes your favorite!

I summed up all the environmental factors that seeds require to first reach germination and then grow into strong, healthy seedlings. As well as the suggested equipment that helps get them there. I feel like it was a lot of information compressed into a short chapter, so here's a quick recap:

- **Humidifiers** increase both the temperature and humidity of the indoor growing room
- **Domes or plastic wrap** keeps the needed moisture from evaporating too quickly
- **Heating mats** warm the soil to germination temperature if the room is too cool
- I stressed that heating mats should be removed as soon as you see sprouts

- Same for the domes and plastic wrap—take them off immediately upon germination
- Try to avoid using heating mats and humidity domes at the same time. Remember, **heat + moisture = mold, mildew, and bacteria**
- Seeds and seedlings need light to thrive. There are many types and styles of **lights** to choose from to accommodate your indoor garden space
- Inexpensive **timers** can be used to schedule your lights so you have one less thing to worry about
- **Oscillating fans** help to circulate the air throughout your indoor garden space and keep things from becoming stagnant and stale. The person who figured out that exposing seedlings to a little air movement to make them grow strong and proud is an absolute genius! The blowing air simulates wind and helps the seedlings more easily adapt to the hardening off process

There are multiple needs that seeds depend on for successful germination. And it's only natural to make mistakes when you first start your gardening journey. Head over to **Chapter 4: Romaine Calm!** and learn the most common problems that most beginner seed-starters have and know ahead of time how you can avoid them! Oh *kale*, yeah!

4

ROMAINE CALM!

COMMON MISTAKES & SOLUTIONS

I WANT YOU TO KNOW HOW PROUD I AM OF YOU FOR WANTING TO start your backyard homestead! I'm so thrilled to be on this adventure with you that I wet my plants!! I actually kinda feel like we're old friends already! How are you feeling so far? Excited? Nervous? A little scared of making mistakes? Ugh, mistakes. I detest that word. As long as you learn from something, can it really be a mistake?

Whether this is your first time trying, or you're just contemplating on giving starting seeds indoors a whirl, or if you've tried it a few times but things didn't work out, I'm proud of you nonetheless. But, I must tell you, mistakes are inevitable. So throughout this chapter, I'm going to tell you about some of the most common problems you may run into as a beginner seed starter and share some of my best practices for starting seeds indoors. As you read through them all, you can romaine calm knowing you're learning how to avoid a total mishap and how to fix things if you make a boo-boo or two.

NOT PROVIDING ENOUGH LIGHT

It's something so simple, yet many people underestimate the importance of making sure their seeds have **12-16 hours of light each day.** Without sufficient light exposure, seedlings will grow a lot slower and might become leggy. Gardeners who don't supply enough light can expect to have longer crop times and a higher rate of seed mortality. Be careful not to confuse the light requirements for **seedlings** with those of **seeds.** These are totally separate issues. Once your seeds germinate, they need light to survive and thrive, there's no doubt there! But before germination happens, most seeds prefer the darkness and actually germinate best in the dark. Being exposed to light too early may even inhibit their ability to germinate at all. This can be confusing, I know. Especially when I tell you that some seeds like begonias, primulas, and coleuses need light to germinate. When I first started my gardening journey, I read the directions on every packet. I'd read and reread them until things became clear. And when that didn't happen, Google quickly became my resourceful best friend.

In Case You Didn't Know: The term "leggy" is used when seedlings grow quickly in height just so they can get closer to the light source. Legginess happens when there's a lack of or uneven access to light. Because they're so intent on growing tall to reach the light, their strength and girth become sacrificed. Their stems grow thin and stretched as they appear tall and somewhat healthy but are actually quite fragile compared to those that have the same height grown under a sufficient light source.

USING TOO LITTLE OR TOO MUCH WATER

Seedlings need water to grow, but because seeds are fragile little creatures, watering can become challenging for a lot of beginner gardeners. The biggest question I had when I first started my journey was "How much water is enough?" My best advice on this is to always keep your seed-starter mix damp but not wet. I recommend 3 ways of doing this:

- Use a **spray bottle** to gently mist your soil every morning. Check it again later in the day and if the soil looks dry, give them another spritz
- Start a mini-greenhouse. Wet the soil enough so that it's wet but not soaked. Then **cover your tray** (or container) with plastic to keep the soil moist. Keep an eye on it every day and if you see the soil looking dry, remove the cover and give it a spritz
- **Bottom-watering.** This process can take between 10-30 minutes as you slowly keep adding water to your trays, allowing time for the soil to soak up the water through the drainage holes in the bottom of your containers. Use your finger to check the top of the soil to ensure moisture has reached the top of the container. Once it's wet on top, drain any excess water from your tray. Test the top of the soil every day to see if the moisture has left the soil. If it has, repeat the bottom-watering process

STARTING SEEDS TOO EARLY IN THE SEASON

Most seedlings are ready to be transplanted outdoors 4-6 weeks after sprouting. You need to plan for this before you start your indoor seed garden, as many plants don't do well in cooler temperatures. Being exposed to cool air or cold soil puts your little gems in unnecessary distress. When plants become stressed, they're more prone to pests and disease, just like humans! How many of you have been more attuned to pests when you're stressed?! Or become ill when you have a weakened immune system? We've all been there. Your seedlings are no different.

If you find you've sown your seeds too early now that the beautiful spring weather you were having has taken a frightfully cold turn, romaine calm! If your plants have quickly grown and need to be transplanted ASAP, but it's too cold outside, you can transplant them into bigger containers indoors. This will allow more space for them to grow strong, healthy roots. The bigger the containers are, the more space you'll need to find inside your home to allocate them to. A major downfall to having big plants in bigger pots is that **bolting** can occur. The plant could think it's reached maturity and start blossoming inside your home.

Planting too early may seem like a good idea, but it can ultimately reduce or destroy your harvest instead of giving it the head start you were hoping for. Here's my list of **the best candidates for starting seeds early indoors:**

- Broccoli
- Cabbage
- Cauliflower
- Celery
- Eggplant
- Leeks
- Onions
- Parsley
- Peppers
- Pumpkins
- Tomatoes

Notice how I have pumpkins on my list? Many people will disagree with me about starting them indoors and would suggest waiting until the temperature is warm enough to plant them directly in your outside garden. Pumpkins take a long time to fully mature, and I don't have a long growing season, so I would suggest starting these guys indoors if you live somewhere with a shorter growing season and you follow the instructions closely for transplanting.

SOWING SEEDS TOO DEEP

Seeds are fussy little beings. Every type of seed has an individual preference for how deep they like to be planted, so it's essential to always read the packet for each seed you sow. Some seeds need light to germinate, while others require complete darkness. The ones that need light generally get sown at the top of your seed-starter mix but don't get completely covered. This is best achieved by pressing on the soil to create a flat, firm surface to lay the seed on. Place the seed on its new bed and gently press it down into the soil, ensuring that it's embedded in the soil but not completely covered (you should still be able to see the seed partially). As long as the seed can see the light, you're golden!

Knowing how deep to plant each seed can be daunting. I speak from experience on that. If you've checked the package and are still unsure, planting shallow is always better than planting too deep. Seeds that get planted too deep will often grow into weak seedlings, if they even germinate at all. Being buried too far into the soil means they aren't getting the light they need to sprout. (8 *Most Common Seed Starting Mistakes* (*FINALLY Starting Seeds*). 2021, February 18)

General Rule of a Green Thumb:
Plant seeds 2-3 times deep as they are wide

EXPOSING SEEDLINGS TO THE OUTDOORS TOO SOON

Seedlings need to be **hardened off** before being transplanted outside. This step is crucial to whether your plants make it through the transplant process or not. Your seedlings can't understand "tough love" and won't do well if you shock them by leaving them outdoors in elements they aren't used to. Being suddenly exposed to wind, rain, sun, and bugs can lead to seedling disaster. Hardening-off is easy to do, but it requires more of your time as it needs to be done gradually to be done right.

I highly recommend using my **1-Week Hardening-off Process.** It's so easy to do, and it works for me every time. Over the course of a week, you'll take your seedlings outside and gradually expose them to the sun and wind. By day 7, they'll be ready to be permanently transplanted outdoors. **In Chapter 8: It's Kind of a Big Dill**, I give you my step-by-step process for hardening off your seedlings. It takes away all the guesswork and sets you up for extraordinary long-term success.

PLANTING TOO MANY SEEDS AT ONCE

This one's a great tip for beginners to keep in mind. I know how exciting it is to dream about all the yummy veggies and beautiful flowers you'd love to grow in your garden. It's soooo easy to get carried away with what I call "the gardener's dream" as you envision rows of lovely greens that you've proudly grown and raised from seed. It's great to be passionate about your new gardening journey. In fact, you need to have that excitement and love to stay dedicated and nurturing! But it's also equally important to be realistic. If you plant too many seeds at once, it becomes harder to maintain them all. Space can quickly become unavailable for them to thrive, and all your hard work and dedication can end up in disappointment from not being able to provide the proper conditions that lead to their success.

If you really want to experience a fantastic variety of seeds early in your endeavor, look for types that you can direct-sow in outdoor containers or directly in your garden bed. These make a great addition to your garden and can be planted as soon as the temperature outside is warm enough. These seeds are usually considered **"short-season"** seeds since they get planted later than the ones that can be started indoors. A few examples of short-season seeds that are fun to grow are *amaranths, cucumbers, summer and winter squash, and watermelon.*

SEEDS NOT BEING KEPT WARM ENOUGH

Seeds need to be kept warm for them to reach germination. Most prefer to be kept between **65-75°F.** This is soil temperature, not room temperature. Don't make the same mistake I did when I first started my indoor garden and assumed that because my house was kept at 67°F that my seeds were cozy too. The soil was cooler than my house temperature, and I didn't even think to test the temperature of the soil. This is where the soil thermometer (or meat thermometer) comes in handy.

If you need a creative way to add extra warmth to your soil because you don't have a heating mat, clear off the top of your refrigerator and store your seed trays there until germination occurs. They seem to just love the heat that radiates from the top of the fridge. Also, heat rises, so if you have an empty shelf somewhere higher up, this is another ingenious place to keep your trays. Wherever you put them, watch for drafts. They're often overlooked when you think you have an ideal spot.

Once germination happens, seedlings are a lot less delicate to fluctuating temperatures and can be moved to their indoor growing area. Though I would still be cautious of drafts.

NOT LABELING YOUR SEEDS

If you sow more than one type of seed, you'll need to **label** your containers appropriately. Remember those cute little white stakes I dreamt about in my intro? Well, you could also use popsicle sticks or plastic cutlery.

Use permanent ink or a grease pencil (what the heck is a grease pencil?! It's an old-style pencil that writes in wax instead of lead, which makes it a more permanent option. Now my question to you is, why do they call it a grease pencil if it's actually wax?) Print the name of the plant along with the date it was sown on your label. Don't just put "tomato". I mean, come on! What kind of tomato are you creating here?

All varieties of tomatoes have different needs. Properly labeling your plants with detail will ensure you give the seed what it needs to germinate. Good labeling also prepares you with sufficient information for your seedlings to grow up tall and strong, and you'll know the right time frame for transplanting outdoors. Even the old pros would be guessing what a seedling is if it wasn't properly labeled.

My grandmother once told me she sowed five different seeds before she started labeling them, so she had to go off memory of what she thought she had planted and where. Yeah, don't do that. Her memory was wrong. Some grew into seedlings, some didn't. And it was because they weren't getting their essential needs met. Now when my grandmother sows seeds, she puts the seed packet right on the container so she knows exactly what to print on her popsicle stick labels.

GIVING UP TOO SOON

Try, try again—things won't always go your way being a beginner seed-starter. You'll make mistakes along the way. And that's OK because there's no greater satisfaction than starting a seed and watching it grow into a beautiful flower or vegetable plant that produces rich, gorgeous colors and succulent veggies. If your seeds don't germinate, reset and try again! If your transplanted vegetable plants or flowers don't grow as they're supposed to, don't give up! Try again next Spring.

Starting your seeds indoors, making sure to provide everything your seeds and seedlings need to germinate, and then transplanting them outdoors when the time and all environmental factors are right is almost like a full-time job! It's not easy! It's like raising a mini family!! But all things worthwhile take hard work, love, and dedication. When you taste your freshly grown peas, green beans, or ripe tomatoes or when you stare proudly at the beautiful flowers that you grew from seed, it will be worth all the frustrations and do-overs that you had to endure to reach success. Hang in there, you've got this newbie! Make peas with it and try, try again.

USING SEEDS THAT ARE OLD OR STALE

You're going to be putting a ton of work into babying your seeds and seedlings, so you shouldn't start off by using seeds that are already past their prime in age and quality. Avoid this seed-starting mistake by choosing fresh seeds. If you come across a packet that's been sitting around your garage for a while, I'd avoid using it as it's probably lost its quality. I have a neat trick that'll tell you if your seeds are viable: Let the seeds soak in a container of water for about 15 minutes or so. At this time, they'll either have sunk to the bottom or they'll be floating. If they've sunk, they're safe to use! But if they're still floating, they shouldn't be used as they'll have a much lower germination rate and will have less strength and vitality if they do grow.

General Rule of a Green Thumb:

When properly stored, seeds can be kept for at least 2-3 years (if not more) depending on the type of seed and how it was stored. You'll learn more about saving seeds in **Chapter 10: Harvesting and Saving Seeds.**

NOT USING A PROPER
SEED-STARTER MIX

Not just any old soil will do here. Nothing beats using a seed-starter mix that's full of all the essentials seeds need to turn into healthy seedlings. Don't use old garden soil. Don't reuse soil from your houseplants. Always start new and fresh. The only time I'd recommend reusing soil is if it's the magical seed-starter mix I talked about in **Chapter 2: Soil or Spoil.** That one's different because you made it and you know what's in it, so it's safe to reuse for another year and then best dumped into your garden or flower beds. If you choose to buy pre-packaged soil, start with a fresh, clean bag that's specifically meant for starting seeds. It will have the right consistency and texture to promote good germination. Starting with a fresh bag will also ensure that it's free of pests or potential disease.

NOT READING SEED PACKETS

Not reading the instructions on a seed packet is like trying a new recipe without reading the shopping list. You end up totally lost and guessing. You may fluke out with an occasional win doing things this way, but it's not the best practice for success. The seed packet has so much valuable information you need to know, like when to start planting your seed, how deep to plant it, the recommended spacing, and timelines for germination! It will often include the approximate rate of germination, which tells you how many seeds will sprout. These rates are never 100% accurate because it also depends on the external environmental factors that you need to provide (heat, light, water, soil, etc.) but it gives you an idea. If the predicted number is below 75%, I usually sow a few extra seeds to increase my chances of having a healthy crop. If the number is higher, two seeds per container is my limit.

Even if you think you know the specifics for a particular veggie or flower, read the packet anyway. Different varieties of the same vegetable or flower could have different needs than the ones you're already familiar with.

(*Don't Make These Common Seed Starting Mistakes.* 2021, December 2)

Avoiding mistakes and problems is something everybody would do if they could. Luckily for you, I gave you a head start on this by listing the most common problems beginners make when starting seeds indoors. Starting seeds too soon, planting too deep, not enough water, too much water, stale seeds... These are just a few of the mishaps you could encounter. But just think, without trial and error, we wouldn't know the right way to be successful so take a second to thank the ones who made these mistakes for us so that we can learn from them. But even if you make a mistake—don't be hard on yourself. Learn from it. *Celerybrate* the wins and be proud of everything you accomplish!

Life is too short to have clean fingernails

5

GETTIN' YOUR HANDS DIRTY

SOIL PREPARATION

WHATEVER SEED-STARTING MIX YOU DECIDE TO USE, PLEASE MAKE sure it's sterile. I can't stress this enough. Non-sterilized, reused, and even some homemade potting soils can contain disease, insects, or weed seeds that can negatively affect the outcome of your plants. Seedlings and mature plants benefit even more from sterile soil because it helps to prevent deadly fungal problems from occurring. Store-bought seed-starter mix or potting soil that's clearly labeled as already being sterilized won't need to be sterilized again before using. But be sure to read that it's sterile as not all store-bought soil comes clean and risk-free.

This is another excellent reason why I love using **the 3 magic ingredients to make my own starter mix.** The peat moss alone is naturally antiseptic, so that takes care of any worries about disease. The perlite provides a sterile filler with a neutral pH to aerate the soil and let oxygen and water easily pass through. The vermiculite is also sterile and will not rot, deteriorate, or mold. This magic formula for seed-starting takes all the hassle out of needing to pre-sterilize your mix. The only time you should ever need to sterilize it is if you were going to reuse it for a second season and you knew the seedlings that were previously in that mix were sick, diseased, or had an insect problem.

Personally, if this happened to me, I wouldn't go through the struggle of sterilizing the soil as I would much rather start a healthy new batch of starter-mix. Sterilizing the soil kills not only harmful fungi and disease, it also removes helpful soil organisms. Heating the soil to 160°F or over will release saturated salts that can be harmful to plants. And last, you'll never be able to look at your stove or microwave the same again. The stink! Oh, the stink!! I thought the smell of skunk was the worst smell ever. That changed the day I tried the whole sterilizing process. I had that smell stuck in my nose hairs all weekend! Yuck!! But hey, to each their own. Some people don't mind the strong......earthy.....smell.

STERILIZING YOUR SOIL

If you really need to sterilize your mix, there are a few ways of sterilizing small batches of soil: The oven method, the microwave method, and the solar energy method. When using any of these methods, you'll need to add in equal parts perlite or vermiculite (if it's not already in your soil) to make sure the soil doesn't get hard.

1) Oven Method: Preheat your oven to 200°F. Spread your soil out in a disposable baking pan up to 4″ deep. Make sure the soil is moist as the steam helps to heat the soil to temperature and penetrate the soil completely. Using dry soil smells even worse than wet soil by the way. Cover the pan using aluminum foil to keep the heat in. Poke a small hole in the foil for your thermometer to go when it's time to test the temperature. The soil needs to reach a temperature of between 160-180°F to start the sterilizing process. Maintain this temperature for at least 30 minutes for the sterilizing to be complete. Allow the soil to cool completely before using.

Side note: I heard you can use a turkey-roasting bag in the oven to contain the smell to just the bag. Not sure if this works—personally, I have no intention of trying.

2) Microwave Method: The microwave method takes less time but works best if you only need a small batch of soil done. I always recommend doing just a pint at a time. Any microwave-safe container with a lid or microwave-safe plastic bag will work as long as you have a small hole for venting the steam. The soil should be moist and you'll still need to maintain a temperature between 160-180°F in the microwave for sterilizing to begin. It usually takes about 15 minutes on high for the soil to reach the temperature. You can use a microwave-safe temperature probe to monitor the temperature as you go. Allow the soil to cool completely before using.

3) Solar Energy Method: I learned this method from my grandmother as it was her go-to way of sterilizing soil when money was tight. She filled clear plastic bags with soil and left them in full sun for a minimum of two weeks. We know in today's world that this method wouldn't have completely sterilized the soil, but it would've killed off certain diseases like damping-off fungi and nematodes.

In Case You Didn't Know: Nematodes (also known as roundworms) are parasitic worms that feed off plants.

Pro Tip! It bothers me so much when I hear people saying, "Oh, I just pour boiling water over my soil to keep it sterile." Um....NO. Pouring boiling water over the soil will not sterilize it at all! What you're doing is killing every microorganism, the good and the bad, so this is not good for your soil. I don't carrot all if it's "easy". It's useless. Don't do this.

CHOOSING YOUR SOIL

Seed-starting mixes and potting soils are not all created equally. Go into any garden center and you'll find bags and bags of the stuff, all from different suppliers and all made with different ingredients. So which one do you choose? While experienced gardeners have their go-to's, beginners may be at a loss of what to use. One thing to keep in mind is that there is a difference between seed-starting mixes and potting soil. Seed-starting mixes don't contain any soil, have a finer texture, and are usually made from a mixture of peat moss (or its substitute), perlite, and vermiculite. I know some people use potting soil to start their seeds, but I don't recommend this. Potting soil has a more coarse texture, it usually contains a fertilizer that can harm delicate seeds, and it doesn't have the nutrients or density that give seeds their ideal growing environment.

So, how do you tell the difference between seed-starting mix and potting soil?

The only way to know the actual difference is by reading the ingredient list. If it's not made up of field soil, compost, or sand, it's a seed-starting mix. If it lists field soil, compost, or sand, then it's potting soil. There are a few visual differences too. Check out this handy chart to understand the difference between seed-starting mix and potting soil. (Hemingway, M. 2019, January 30).

Seed-Starting Mix:

- Contains a combination of peat moss, coconut coir, perlite, or vermiculite
- Finer in texture than potting soil (this makes it easier for roots to flow freely)
- It doesn't contain any actual soil
- It's lightweight so it doesn't weigh seeds down

Potting Soil:

- Usually contains field soil, compost, or sand, though it may have perlite or vermiculite added
- Contains larger particles (making it harder for roots to pass through)
- Coarser in texture than seed-starting mix
- Denser than seed-starting mix
- Usually includes some sort of fertilizer (which often results in being too rich in nutrients)

With so many options claiming they're the best, which one do you choose?

Seed-starter mixes and potting soils both range in price and promise. Being able to sort through them all takes time and can be very over-whelming for the beginner seed-starter. And who wants that? Being an informed buyer can save you time, money, and the hassle of making the wrong choice. I will always stand by using a seed-starter mix over using potting soil for seed-starting. And not just any seed-starting mix. For the best results, I highly recommend using the starter-mix with the 3 magic ingredients listed in **Chapter 2: Soil or Spoil.**

. . .

If, after reading this, you'd still rather use a bagged mix before even attempting to make your own, **here are a few things to watch out for when selecting your mix:**

- If the bag doesn't list its ingredients, this is a hard pass. The last thing you want is a starter-mix or soil made with unknown products
- If it contains "forest products", skip it. These are dense fillers found in lower-quality seed-starter mixes
- Mixes that contain fertilizer or lime should not be used. The proper mixture already contains enough nutrients from its peat moss(or its substitute), perlite, and vermiculite to give the seeds a good start. Any added fertilizer would be too much as it could burn or damage the seeds
- Look for bags that are light and dry. If you come across bags that are damp or heavy, keep walking. Chances are they may have become compacted (instead of being light and fluffy) and could contain sand
- Make sure it promotes good drainage and water retention
- Has a pH between 5-6.5 (having an unbalanced pH level means there's too much or too little alkaline or too much or too little acid in the soil. Unbalanced pH levels can hinder your seedlings growth as they aren't able to fully use the nutrients and minerals in the soil)
- Allows good airflow

THE IMPORTANCE OF PRE-MOISTENING YOUR SEED-STARTER MIX

Pre-moistened soil is fabulous in so many ways. First, it allows your mix to easily accept its first few rounds of watering. This is important because some mixes don't retain water as readily as others do. If you plant seeds in dry soil, the mix will actually repel the water instead of retain it. The water will end up beading and running across the top of the soil and can literally wash your seeds away. This can lead to a confusing seed mash-up as they flow out of the holes that you measured and poked so perfectly. Seed types could mix, resulting in mistaking seeds for what they actually are and sowing them too deep or too shallow. This is a big no-no for germination.

When you pre-moisten your mix before packing it into containers, you'll notice that everything becomes more manageable. When it comes time to water your freshly planted seeds, the water will soak right in. The soil will be open and porous just like a wet sponge. Have you ever put a dry sponge in water? It'll just sit there and float, right? Not doing its job, not holding any water. But what happens to an already damp sponge? That sucker will absorb water so quickly it'll be soaking wet before you know it! Your start-mix works the same way.

Another good reason for pre-wetting your soil is to settle all of its particles. When you pack your pre-moistened mix into containers, you'll notice it all holds together nicely and flattens better. Try to pack and flatten dry soil and you'll find it frustrating as it continues bouncing back up and not holding as nothing is binding it together.

Lastly—air pockets. Dry soil is usually full of them, and we don't want that. They prevent the soil from binding, making you think you have more soil in your containers than you actually do. Over time, the soil will settle and you'll see that you've lost precious volume that seeds need to thrive in. Those air pockets will prevent water from dispersing throughout the soil and can lead to a very unhappy, unwatered seed.

The best way to moisten your mix is by dumping it into a pail large enough to allow for some good stirring. Next, you're going to add water. I usually pour rain or distilled water in a little at a time to make sure I don't add too much at once. It's easier to add water if the soil is still too dry than to remove it if it becomes too wet (if you add too much water, don't worry—this can be fixed by adding more mix to the bucket). You'll be able to tell by the color and texture of the soil if more water is needed. I usually add water until my handfuls of darkened soil hold together nicely, with no excess water draining when I squeeze a tight ball between my fingers. Another way to know when it's ready is when the texture reminds you of playing with wet sand. It may take several minutes of stirring and adding to reach this consistency as anything peat-based is slower to absorb moisture.

Once your soil reaches this consistency, you're ready to fill your containers. If you haven't already done so, make sure each container or cell has a hole in the bottom to allow for drainage and bottom-watering. If there's no hole, use a knife to make a small one about the width of a straw. When planting seeds indoors, you'll want to make sure your work-space is protected, as this part can get a little messy. I usually put an old baking sheet under my containers to catch any excess soil that may spill when filling my containers. You could also use your reservoir tray and just dump any excess soil before adding your containers or cells.

FILLING YOUR CONTAINERS WITH SOIL

Add enough soil to each cell or tray so when you pack it down, it's about ¾'s full. Using your fingers, press the soil until it's nice and firm, making sure all the corners are filled nicely. Add a little more mix to the tops of your containers, press it down tight, and now you're ready to sow your seeds (we'll go into detail on this in **Chapter 6: Party Thyme**).

FILLING YOUR RESERVOIR WITH WATER AND SOAKING YOUR CAPILLARY MAT

Now it's time to set your seeds up for bottom-watering. It's always best to use rain or distilled water when filling your reservoir or trays. Rainwater is filled with natural nutrients that plants thrive on—sodium, potassium, calcium, magnesium, and many others. If rainwater isn't available to you yet, distilled water can be used in its place, but one thing to keep in mind is that distilled water has no nutrients. It contains nothing but pure H2O. So if you choose to use distilled water, you'll need to pair it with a supplement (after germination) that'll provide adequate nutrients so that you don't run into a calcium or magnesium deficiency.

Don't get me wrong, tap water is always an option as well. Many have used it, myself included, and have had decent results. But if you're looking for the best options with the best results, stick with rain or distilled water.

You can save some money by making your own distilled water. All you need is a large pot filled with about 1/3rd water, a heat-resistant container to set inside the pot, a lid, and some ice. Start by bringing your water to a boil with the lid sitting upside down on top of the pot. Add a couple of ice cubes to the lid to keep the lid cool so the condensation from the steam boiling from the water condenses on the cool lid and drips into the container that's set inside the pot. This can be a very slow time-consuming process as you only get about 8 ounces of distilled water per hour. But if you have the time and enjoy doing as much DIY as possible, making your own distilled water is an impressive addition to becoming a self-sufficient backyard homesteader.

If you're using the capillary mat system, fill your reservoir with water. Your capillary mat is also known as a **wicking mat** that sits on a stand inside the tray with one end of the mat sitting directly in the water. The wicking mat is made of absorbent material, usually felt or wool, and provides a great base for your seed containers to rest on as they become self-sufficient and efficiently draw up the water when needed. Always make sure that your reservoir has enough water for your mat to always stay wet.

Keep in mind that wicking mats are reusable, but only to a point. Sometimes roots get intertwined in the felt or seedlings become sick. This is when you'd want to change your mat. Make sure you buy actual capillary mat felt that's 100% wool or polyester and not craft or recycled felt when it comes time to replace because the additives found in crafting or recycled felt can't be washed out and are not good for your plants.

. . .

If you're feeling adventurous, I have a fun DIY project for making your own self-wicking mat. You'll need a few supplies to get started:

- Plastic tray
- Scissors
- Styrofoam (about the size of your tray and approximately 1″ thick)
- A piece of 100% wool fabric (an old sweater, blanket, or scarf works perfectly)
- Nails or thumbtacks
- Containers or cells to fill your plastic tray
- Water

Creating Your Self-Wicking System:

- Place your foam inside the tray, allowing for about 1″ of space all around
- Cut your wool to cover the styrofoam, leaving extra wool on the ends to lie in and absorb the water
- Nail or tack the wool to the styrofoam to keep it in place
- Place the covered styrofoam wool side up in the tray
- Fill the tray with water. Make sure the wool is wet but not sitting completely underwater. It will naturally wick up the water as needed as long as you have the two ends hanging down touching the water
- Arrange your containers or cells on top of the wool-covered styrofoam and let them be self-sufficient as they soak up as much water as they need whenever they need it
- Monitor the water level in your tray. It usually lasts several days, up to a week before needing to be filled
- Always be sure that your containers or cells are never sitting directly in the water. This leads to mold or rotting and is no good for your little gems

Throughout Chapter 5, I discussed a few ways of gettin' your hands dirty. I talked about using sterile ingredients when making your seed-starting mix and how to ensure your store-bought mix is **sterile**. I went through a few methods of the how-to's on sterilizing your mix if you ever need to. You learned **the difference between potting soil and starter-mix** and what to look for when shopping for them. You also learned the importance of **wetting your mix before packing it** in your containers or cells and why it could make or break your efforts if you don't. Wet soil allows you to put the right amount of mix in your containers or cells the first time so you don't disrupt the seeds and soil absorbs water so much easier when it's already moist. Planting in dry soil will affect the depth the seeds need to germinate in because once the soil gets watered, it will settle and the volume of soil will change. Needing to add extra soil to compensate for the lack of volume will result in burying the seed too deep. Using a **capillary mat system** is a great way to bottom-water your seeds and seedlings. This system takes the guesswork out of how much water to give. The soil will naturally draw whatever water it needs right from the mat. As long as the reservoir has water to keep the mat wet, you're good to let them be! When it comes time to change the capillary mat, make sure you buy the real thing. Don't skimp out by using craft or recycled felt—their additives are harmful to your little gems and usually end up as a wasted batch.

Coolest garden

6

PARTY THYME

SOWING SEEDS

HOW TO PROPERLY PLANT YOUR SEEDS TO REACH GERMINATION

THE BEST ADVICE I CAN GIVE YOU ON THIS, AND I CAN'T STRESS IT enough, is to read the package. There you'll find how deep your seeds should be planted. Some seeds need full light to germinate, while others prefer being completely in the dark. The ones that need light generally get sown at the top of your seed-starter mix and don't get completely covered with soil. Some small seeds can be scattered directly on top of the soil, while most larger seeds will need to be buried. Seeds that are planted too deep can grow into fragile seedlings, and that's if they even germinate at all. Depth matters! How your soil gets packed in your containers, which seeds you choose from the packet, watering, labeling, and covering—it all matters.

FILLING YOUR CONTAINERS

Ok, now that you have your seed-starting mix ready to go, and all your packets full of important juicy information, it's time to fill your containers with starter mix. Make sure your soil mix is moist (but not soaking wet), then fill and pack your containers, ensuring there aren't any gaps amongst the layers of soil. Now you're ready to plant your seeds! Yay!

Pro Tip! When packing your containers, think of it like how you would pack brown sugar into a measuring cup. You need to pack it so that there aren't any spaces or air gaps that would throw off your measurement. BUT don't pack it so tight that you don't have some spring to the soil mix. You should be able to press gently with a flattened finger, and the soil mix should bounce right back. Make sense?? Give it a try!

ARRANGING YOUR SEEDS

So you've ripped open and read the seed package, now what? Now it's time to choose the best seeds from the package. I'm partial to the largest seeds of the bunch as they usually have the best chance at germination. This doesn't mean the smaller ones won't germinate, so don't go tossing them out just because they're little. They could end up germinating perfectly fine, but since you're starting with just a few seeds from the package, it's best to choose the ones that give you the best odds of thriving.

When deciding on where to sow your seeds, I find it helpful to create little indents in the soil to plan out where each seed will go. You can use the tip of your pinky finger or the eraser on a pencil to make your divots. Once you place your seeds according to the required depth on their package, sprinkle some fresh soil over the top of each hole and pat down gently to cover. You want to be sure that the seeds that require covering are well covered and the seeds that require light are just barely tucked in by the mix.

SEED DEPTH

I still read my seed packages today and you should too. I know that sometimes packages get misplaced or maybe you've been given some loose seeds by a friend or neighbor and aren't able to read the proper sowing instructions. If this happens, you'll need to get all the valuable information needed to increase your chances of reaching germination and developing hardy seedlings. The exact depth differs between seed types, sometimes even when they're from the same family! A lot of seed packages suggest planting seeds a ¼" deep. However, this is considered too deep for the tiny seed varieties. If you can't find the proper depth instructions for your particular type of seed, the rule is to not plant any seed deeper than 2-3 times its diameter. Planting too shallow is always better than planting too deep.

Pro Tip! You can sprinkle tiny seeds (like carrots or leaf lettuce) directly on the top of the seed-starter mix and then just barely cover them with soil.

Here's my handy cheat sheet for the sowing depth of a few of my favorite crops:

- Beets ½"
- Cabbage ¼" (I sprinkle these)
- Carrots ¼" (sprinkle)
- Cauliflower ½"
- Corn 1.5"
- Cucumbers ½"
- Garlic 2"

- Kale ½"
- Leaf Lettuce ¼" (sprinkle)
- Melons ½"
- Onions ¼" (sprinkle)
- Peas 1.5"
- Pumpkins 1"
- Radishes ½"
- Tomatoes ⅛"

I like to sow two seeds per cell. I do this to double my chances of germination, plus I know that not all seeds have an equal germination rate. The average germination rate for vegetable seeds is 90%. This means if you plant a 72-cell starter tray with one seed per cell, only about 65 of those seeds will germinate (72 x 90%). When I sow two seeds per cell, I double those odds.

Your seeds will germinate, but they all won't germinate equally. If both seeds in a cell germinate (which often they do as you can see by the odds), you'll need to choose the healthier of the two and snip the other. Sometimes you'll have a seed shoot up really quick but become leggy. This wouldn't be considered a hardy plant to choose to keep, but if it were the only one in the cell, then it'd be worth keeping. BUT if you had a second plant in the same cell come up a little slower and it's looking a little greener, your best bet would be to keep the later one and snip the leggy one. When I first started my pumpkins, I was totally clueless about legginess. I believed the opposite was true for keeping plants. I made the mistake of thinking that the quicker, taller ones were doing so much better than the delayed, shorter ones and ended up snipping the healthier ones. I still feel bad to this day just thinking about it! What was I thinking?! And that wasn't even my biggest mistake! You know how there are exceptions to almost every rule? Well, that applies to sowing two seeds per cell as well.

General Rule of a Green Thumb:

Increase your chances of germination by planting two seeds per cell UNLESS you're planting larger seeds. Melons, squash, or PUMPKINS should be planted with only one seed per cell. But common vegetables like onions, beets, peas, and radishes can be sown in sprinkles of three to five seeds per cell as they can grow as a cluster of seedlings.

Oh, the mistakes I made. I can't help but chuckle at myself now. I was such an innocent, avid gardener. I made mistakes, but it was OK because I had fun. I didn't know any better. My leggy pumpkins still grew into beautiful plants with strong roots and leaves, but many of them didn't end up flowering at all. Live and learn.

Snipping healthy-looking seedlings isn't as easy as it sounds but I've learned that just because I started growing them, that doesn't mean I should keep them all. Keeping two plants per cell can lead to more harm than good. The stronger one ends up having to share its moisture and nutrients with the weaker one, which takes away vital elements for making the stronger one even stronger and more robust. Do yourself the favor and make the cut.

WATERING YOUR SEEDS

Now that you've got your seeds all planted, it's time to break out the spray bottle. Let's give these babies some much-needed moisture! Give each pot a few spritzes, enough to wet the soil. We don't want them soaked, but we want them wet. Alternatively, you can use a clean turkey baster to let the water drip onto each cell without disrupting the soil or dislodging the seeds. This works a little quicker than the spray bottle method, but I find I have more control using the mist. Sure it takes longer, but what's the rush? You've already dedicated this much time. Regardless of whether you use the spray bottle or the turkey baster, you'll want to go over your containers or cells a couple of times to make sure they're adequately wet.

. . .

You can now choose to bottom-water your seeds. Bottom-watering is watering your plants from the bottom up. When plants take in their water directly from the bottom of the soil, they have stronger roots. This is likely because they're growing down directly towards the moisture. Bottom-watering can be time consuming, but if you're interested in trying this method, I'd suggest re-reading Chapter 5: Gettin' Your Hands Dirty. I went into great detail about how to bottom-water using the capillary mat method. There's even a cool DIY recipe on how to make your own self-wicking mat.

To bottom-water without a capillary mat, add water to the tray holding your containers or cells. There's usually too much plant-damaging chlorine in tap water, so stick to distilled or rainwater. Bottom-watering can take between 10-30 minutes as you slowly keep adding water to your tray, allowing time for the soil to soak up the water through the drainage holes in the bottom of your containers. Use your finger to check the top of the soil to ensure moisture has reached the top of the container. Once it's wet on top, drain any excess water from your tray. Test the top of the soil daily to see if the moisture has left the top of the soil. If it has, repeat the bottom-watering process. (O'Donnell, J. 2020, April 7)

LABELING YOUR SEEDS

Time for labeling! If you're planting more than one type of seed, which you and I both know you will be, you need to properly label your containers. Permanent markers work great on popsicle sticks, plant stakes, or even plastic cutlery. Find something that works for you. Anything goes as long as it lasts and provides you with enough room to write the basic information for each seed. I strongly suggest putting **the name of your plant, date sown, time frame for germination**, and if you have room, add the plant and row spacing to make it easier when it comes time to transplant them in your outdoor garden.

COVERING YOUR SEED TRAYS

To cover or not to cover, that is the question... To give the germination process a boost, you can use plastic wrap or a clear plastic dome to cover your containers to keep the moisture in. This isn't a necessity to reach success, your seeds can germinate no problem without a dome or cover. But keeping the moisture in has benefits when starting seeds indoors:

- Since the covering acts like a mini-greenhouse, you can expect to have quicker germination rates. Seeds like tomatoes and peppers germinate faster with warmer soil temperatures. (*Epic Gardening*. 2019, March 3)
- Higher germination rates. A humidity dome or plastic wrap keeps the warmth and moisture inside the tray. These are ideal soil conditions for most seeds to germinate in. A higher germination rate is beneficial when trying to grow older seeds
- Plastic domes usually come in standard sizes to fit a 24, 36, or 72 cell tray. They also come in different shapes to accommodate your growing needs—round, rectangular, or square. You can make your own by cutting clear plastic bottles or clear plastic food containers. Any bottle or container will do as long as they're clear to let the light through.

If you'd rather use plastic wrap instead of a dome, poke a few holes in the plastic with a toothpick to allow for some ventilation. Mold will undoubtedly grow if your containers can't breathe at all. Check your soil twice per day for moisture. You can usually tell how wet they are by the color of the soil. Darker soil means they're still moist. Let the soil surface dry between waterings. Once you spot some little green sprouts, remove the plastic and watch them grow, grow, grow! It's so important to remove the dome as soon as you see germination has occurred. The last thing you want is to have mold or fungus growing on your seedlings.

· · ·

When I first experimented with growing pumpkins under a plastic dome, I made the mistake of leaving the dome on slightly past the sprouting stage. I figured I had to wait until all my pots showed some green. I was wrong. I ended up with white mold growing on the top of the soil from too much humidity and too much moisture.

General Rule of a Green Thumb:
When in doubt, watch for sprout!
As soon as you see little green sprouts, it's time to celebrate!
Germination has occurred!

This chapter gave you my entire step-by-step method of sowing seeds from start to finish.

- I told you how and how not to **pack your containers with the seed-starter mix**
- Bigger isn't always better, but it appears true for seeds **—choose the biggest ones to have the best success**
- Depth matters when it comes to sowing—some seeds need light and some don't want light at all, so **follow the instructions on the packet when sowing your seeds**
- Be sure to keep the germination odds in your favor and **sow two seeds per cell.** This doesn't apply when planting larger seeds like melons, squash, and pumpkins. For these, one will do
- **The initial watering after sowing is important.** No matter how you pack your mix in the cell or container, it will still settle a bit after its first watering. What you don't want happening is disruption or displacement of the seed you just sowed
- Be careful and gentle if you're watering from the top. If you're afraid of the seeds moving or the soil covering getting

disturbed, then it's best to **use a misting spray bottle.**
There's no way a gentle mist will spoil your sowing efforts!
So what if it takes a little longer?!

- **Bottom-watering** is a popular method that won't disturb
  your seeds but remember—if your seed is right at the top of
  the mix, then you'll want to spray it from above as well to
  wet the surface

- **Labeling** doesn't sound all that important, but it truly is.
  You'll need to know the name, date sowed, time frame for
  germination, and spacing measurements for transplanting.
  Having all that information handy with your seed
  containers makes your caretaking job a lot easier. No
  guessing or searching for the seed packet, no need to say
  "Hey Google, how long do I have to wait before I see some
  dang sprouts?!"

- I talked about your options for using a **humidity dome
  or plastic wrap** and how both options keep your seed
  mix damp and stop the moisture from evaporating into the
  room air. But what it can also do is breed mold. The cover
  should not fit airtight. Rest it on the seed tray to allow a little
  circulation of air. Some covers have an adjustable vent you
  can open or close to control the humidity. If using plastic
  wrap, poke some holes after wrapping. It'll still help hold
  most of the moisture in without it getting too humid. As
  soon as you notice sprouts, remove the cover or take out the
  cells that have sprouted and leave the rest to germinate.

You've read this far, so I know you're committed to learning the best
method for starting your seeds indoors. The old saying goes "work smart,
not hard". And that's precisely what you'll be doing if you follow my
lead. Don't get me wrong, it's still a lot of work! But I've taken my experience and the experience that my grandmother has passed on to me and
put it into this book so that you can have an excellent start to a life full of
self-sufficiency. Or at the very least, a healthy garden full of strong,
healthy plants and flowers.

By now you'll have a general idea of how to prepare your seeds for germination. Thyme to turnip the beet as we move on to more in-depth learning about the actual germination process in **Chapter 7: Let It Grow, Let It Grow!** (Can't hold me back anymore...)

My Garden Feeds My Soul

7

LET IT GROW, LET IT GROW!

GERMINATION

Put your technical thinking caps on while reading this chapter, as I'm about to give you a more detailed explanation of the germination process. I'll be using a few advanced words in terms of gardening jargon, but rest assured, I've included definitions for many of the new terms I'm using. I didn't want this to turn into textbook reading, but I feel it's essential to have a basic understanding of how a seed works and the amazing changes it goes through to produce a beautiful, robust plant!

A seed consists of three parts: **the embryo, endosperm, and seed coat.**

The **embryo** is the youngest part of the seed from which a new plant will grow once its ideal growing conditions have been met. The **endosperm** is the stored food (mainly starches) that the embryo needs to stay alive. Lastly, the **seed coat** is the outer lining of the seed. It's usually made up of one or many layers, and its job is to protect the inside of the seed.

There are 5 stages in a seed's germination process:

1. The seed absorbs water through its pores (the technical term for this is **"imbibition"**)
2. The **water stimulates enzymes** that start the plant's growth
3. The **seed grows a root** that accesses water through the soil
4. The **seed produces shoots** that grow towards the light source
5. The shoots produce leaves and the **photomorphogenesis process begins**

In Case You Didn't Know: "In developmental biology, Photomorphogenesis is light-mediated development, where plant growth patterns respond to the light spectrum. This is a completely separate process from photosynthesis, where light is used as a source of energy. The photomorphogenesis of plants is often studied by using tightly frequency-controlled light sources to grow the plants. There are at least three stages of plant development where photomorphogenesis occurs: seed germination, seedling development, and the switch from the vegetative to the flowering stage" (Wikipedia contributors. 2020, December 7)

DORMANCY—AWAKENING THE SLEEPING GIANT

Germination brings the seed out of its dormant state. Remember how I talked about seeds being "alive" but in an inactive state until planted? During germination, the seed's embryo absorbs water to start the photomorphogenesis process which hydrates and expands its cells. This alerts the seed that it's time to begin certain processes that were reduced during its dormancy. Its respiration will increase and various metabolic functions will resume. This all happens because the seed goes through structural changes in the cells of its embryo. Sometimes germination will start early in the development process and will go one of two ways:

1. The seed's embryo will develop within the ovule, forcing out a swollen root through a flower that's still attached! In peas and corn, the cotyledons (seed leaves) stay beneath the soil. This type of germination is called **hypogeal germination.**

2. Beans and sunflowers go through **epigeal germination,** which means the germination process takes place all above ground. In epigeal germination, stems may grow several inches above ground, bringing the seed leaves with them out into the light. This is when they'll begin turning green and have a leaf-like appearance.

In Case You Didn't Know: A cotyledon (the first leaf or two) "is a significant part of the embryo within the seed of a plant and is defined as "the embryonic leaf in seed-bearing plants, one or more of which are the first to appear from a germinating seed." The number of cotyledons present is one characteristic used by botanists to classify the flowering plants (angiosperms). Species with one cotyledon are called monocotyledonous ("monocots"). Plants with two embryonic leaves are termed dicotyledonous ("dicots")." (Wikipedia contributors. 2021, March 7).

The dormant state differs from seed to seed. For some, dormancy is brief. This means when the seed reaches its optimal environmental conditions (temperature, light, and moisture), it will germinate and the embryo will resume growth. Some seeds require their dormant state to be broken. Even if they've achieved their preferred environmental conditions, they will not germinate until they've had a change in their seed coat or embryo. The embryo itself usually has no dormancy and can develop once the seed coat is removed or has shed enough of its lining to let water in. In these cases, germination relies on the rotting or softening of the seed coat from the moisture in the soil. When the seed coat is tough and thick, you can give it some help by putting a small nick in the seed's shell before planting. This process is known as **scarification. Scarification** makes it so much easier for the seed to absorb water through its heavy coat. If you don't give it a nick, germination will depend on the coat weakening naturally by decomposition and continued softening from the moisture. These processes take time, so germination will take longer to begin. Most vegetable seeds are naturally soft and don't require scarification, but a select few like beans, pumpkin, spinach, and squash all have tough coats and should be nicked and soaked before planting. Some varieties of flowers like morning glories or nasturtiums have tough coats as well.

THE BEST METHOD FOR SCARIFYING YOUR SEEDS

You'll need a few necessary tools, most of which can be found around your home. I recommend having sandpaper and a file handy, each used for different types and sizes of seeds. I like using a file on bigger seeds like morning glories and sandpaper on the smaller ones like nasturtiums. The best way to use sandpaper is by rubbing seeds together in between two sheets. After you have your tools ready, you'll need a few bowls (depending on how many seeds you're doing), room temperature water, and if you need to do scarification followed by stratification then you'll need some peat moss and plastic baggies for storing overnight.

In Case You Didn't Know: Stratification is the process of creating a cool, moist environment to break dormancy and promote germination. This is most often achieved by placing seeds close together in layers of moist sand or peat moss. This aids in preservation and germination. Cold stratification is supposed to mimic the conditions of a cold, wet spring as the seeds are surrounded in cool, moist soil. Seeds that benefit from stratification are usually small and tiny perennials. Lettuce seed, milkweed, and perennial sunflowers have higher germination rates when exposed to cold stratification before spring planting. Even when they're started indoors!

Once you've gathered your tools, you're ready to start scarifying!

1. Use your preferred tool to **gently nick the seed coat just enough so that the inside shows through**. The inside of a seed is usually a lighter color than the outer layer. Be extra careful to not damage the seed. As soon as the inside shows, you're done with that seed
2. **Continue the nicking process for all of your seeds**
3. Once they've all been nicked, **soak the seeds in room temperature water, leaving them overnight.**
4. Once the seeds swell, they become time-sensitive, so **take them out of the water immediately and sow them in your seed-starter mix as soon as possible**
5. If you're using the **stratification process**, layer the seeds in damp peat moss in a sealed plastic baggie and store them in the fridge. Some seeds only need to stay cool overnight while others, like poppy seed, require several weeks, so check your packages carefully

For many seeds, even under perfect environmental conditions, germination won't happen until a certain time frame has passed. This time allows for the necessary embryonic development of the seed.

TEMPERATURE

The germination process might be slightly different for each seed, but their needs are close enough so that you can still grow most of them together. The desired temperature range is between 65-75°F for most seeds, which is easily maintained by either raising the temperature on your house thermostat, adding a small heater to your growing area, or by using a heat mat. The heat mat is the most sustainable option since it will heat just the soil and not the room or the house. Tomatoes and peppers like warm soil, so if you group them together, the mat can be placed under that specific section of your seed-starter system. Keep in mind that you'll need to remove or unplug the mat as soon as you see sprouts. It's only needed for the seeds to reach germination.

WATER

The correct amount of water is crucial for germination. The cells need to be **kept damp but not overly wet**. As we talked about in **Chapter 6: Party Thyme**, bottom-watering with or without a capillary mat, careful top watering using the turkey baster, or a spray bottle with a gentle mist can accomplish this. The seed shells need to soften enough to let the first leaves out, so to keep the moisture from evaporating into the room you can use a humidity dome or plastic wrap (also talked about in **Chapter 6: Party Thyme**). **Once you see sprouts remove the humidity dome or plastic wrap.** Leaving it on any longer will promote mold and mildew to grow on the surface of the soil. If you're using a heating mat, skip the dome. Using both can harm your seeds.

LIGHT

Only some seeds need light to germinate, but all seedlings need light to grow through the process of photosynthesis. You should have a plan where you will set your pots for as much light as they can get. If you don't have the room you need at a south-facing window, then you'll need some artificial light to get your seeds going. **Fluorescent light fixtures are best to use.** You can purchase seed-starter systems that come with a light, or if your system is more of a DIY, then a 2 or 4-foot secondhand fixture found at your local reuse-it store is the perfect alternative. You can easily hang the fixture from chains to maintain close positioning to the top of the containers or cells and raise the fixtures as your seedlings grow taller. Setting a timer to turn the lights off and on automatically can make your life a little easier. For germination, you can set the time to mimic the light of a beautiful spring day, which would be about 12 hours. Once they germinate, they can have up to 18 hours of light but still need a period of darkness to feed themselves. (Back To Reality. 2017, March 7)

My grandmother had a funny lighting mishap one year. My grandfather was always a jack-of-all-trades kind of guy. He knew a lot about a lot of things. He despised calling in a tradesperson to fix anything because he swore he could fix most things himself... and usually he did. Quite well. My grandmother had wanted to grow her seed-starting hobby but didn't have adequate space upstairs to expand. She spent days trying to come up with ideas on how to increase her space.

Finally, she decided to clean up the basement (that was primarily being used for storage) and move her growing area downstairs. The lower level wasn't very big, and she certainly didn't have the natural lighting as she had upstairs, so she had to get creative. She got her hands on a couple of used 4-foot fluorescent fixtures that her church had replaced and surprised my grandfather by bringing them home. She asked him to arrange for an electrician to come by to install an electrical outlet near her growing table. She also wanted the fixtures to be fitted with a cord that would plug right into the outlet.

Of course, he responded by saying,

"An electrician? Heck, I can do that myself and it won't cost a dang thing".

My grandmother, knowing better than to argue, told him to give it a shot. He got to working on it the next day. At the end of the second day, he proudly called my grandmother downstairs to show her what he had done. She was thrilled! The fixtures were all lit and hanging by chains, just as she requested. She could simply raise and lower them just by adjusting the hooks on the chains. My grandfather couldn't help but tease her once again,

"There's no need for tradespeople in this house".

When it was time to start her seeds, my grandmother got to work and soon after, she had her containers planted and sitting comfortably under the newly installed lights. She was so excited to see what this new setup would bring. Every day she went downstairs and checked on her gems. She unplugged the lights at the end of each night and plugged them back in each morning. She made sure they all had enough water and started counting down the days until she would see sprouts. She got a little concerned when after seven days her lettuce had not yet sprouted. After ten days there was still no lettuce in sight! She thought,

"What's going on? I know this lettuce has a germination period of 7-10 days. Something's wrong!"

Two days later her broccoli and cauliflower had sprouted as they should, but still no lettuce. She assumed she planted old or bad lettuce seeds, so she went out and replaced them. She replanted and waited another ten days. Still no lettuce. Now she's noticing that after all the time that had passed, her other sprouted seeds were not doing very well at all. They were tiny and skinny and looked very weak. This had never happened in large batches before. So she chalked it up to being a bad batch of seed-starter mix and begrudgingly admitted that she'd have to start all over again.

Time was running out for the season, so she had to get moving or else she wouldn't be able to start from seed. Off to the garden center she went and bought all new seed-starter mix and fresh packets of seeds. When she got home and attempted to go downstairs, her hands were too full to turn on the basement light switch, but she knew she had left the fluorescents plugged in so she wasn't afraid of tripping and falling in the dark. She got to the bottom of the stairs, turned the corner, and saw that the basement was practically black! She dropped her supplies and went back upstairs to turn on the switch. She went back down and discovered the fluorescents were now on. Quite confused, she went upstairs once more to turn the master switch off. Sure enough, off went the fluorescents.

It turned out that the electrical circuit that my grandfather used to power the outlet for my grandmother's beloved fluorescent fixtures was the same as the light switch for the basement light!! So every time my poor grandmother went upstairs and innocently turned off the basement light switch, her fluorescents would also go out. No wonder her lettuce didn't sprout and her seedlings were frail... they had NO light! Needless to say, my grandfather ended up calling an electrician over to fix his mistake. After adding up the cost of new seedling mix, fresh seeds, the wasted time and the electrician, it was a lot more expensive than getting it done right the first time. Ahhh, my grandfather. Jack-of-all-trades, master of none.

Alrighty then! You just passed the technical terms and training part of my lesson! Congratulations! You're on your way to becoming a pro-gardener! While it's not so vital that you remember these words and definitions, I'd rather your takeaway be that a seed is alive. It lies dormant, waiting for YOU to help bring it to life by providing it with what it needs to grow and reproduce. Your job as a gardener is to **provide the seed with proper temperature, light (or no light), and water.** You want the seed to do more than just germinate, of course. But in this chapter, we focused specifically on the miracle of germination and how Mother Nature made things different for some seeds. Some have seed coats so thick that they need help letting moisture in, so we help by thinning their coat with a file or sandpaper. Or, how some seeds need to be fooled out of their dormancy by subjecting them to cooler temperatures to make them think they went through a chilly spring in the ground and are now ready to germinate. I'm sure glad someone figured these things out, or we'd be going through batches of seeds like crazy, thinking we're doing something wrong! Speaking of doing something wrong.....my grandmother says it was probably the gossipers at the church that spread the word about what my grandfather did with the lights. The entire community knew about it and teased him for years, earning him the nickname "Sparky".

What happens
IN THE GARDEN
stays IN THE
garden

8

IT'S KIND OF A BIG DILL

NURTURING YOUR SEEDLINGS

PICTURE THIS. AFTER WEEKS OF PREPARATION AND LOADS OF attention, all your hard work and dedication are finally paying off. You walk into your indoor garden area and your heart swells with pride as you see a variety of green sprouts, all standing tall and proud, waiting to start their outdoor adventure as soon as they can be transplanted outside. They're almost as excited as you are!! Both you and those tiny sprouts may think they're ready, but the truth is they still require some good care before heading outdoors. This means more than just making sure they're watered. This is the time where you need to watch out for things like damping-off, room temperature, moisture level, and amount of light given to your growing gems.

After seeds go through the 5 stages of germination, the plant will begin its journey through **the 6 stages of growth.** The life of a plant can be as short as a few weeks to a few months, and they go through some noticeable changes as they grow, just like humans do! As people, we progress from infant, toddler, adolescent, young adult, middle-aged adult to senior citizen. Plants have a similar cycle that takes them through the stages of sprout, seedling, vegetative, budding, flowering, and ripening. In both cases, there are nutritional needs that change and vary according to the stage of life.

1. **Sprout:** When the seeds have all the nutrients and environmental factors needed to germinate and grow their first pair of true leaves
2. **Seedling:** As roots develop and spread throughout the starter mix, the soil gives your plant a boost as the seedling quickly absorbs the nutrients that provide quick growth from a thin, lanky seedling to a full, robust plant
3. **Vegetative:** This is when the plant becomes focused on growing its stalks and foliage. Nitrogen, an important component of chlorophyll (the green pigment present in all plants) is a key nutrient for plant growth
4. **Budding:** This is the start of a plant's reproductive cycle. The nutrient phosphorus is in high demand as the plant strengthens from growing leaves to developing buds
5. **Flowering:** During this stage, plants start developing healthy flowers and fruit. Potassium is an integral component as it produces and transports all the sugars and starches that plants need to fully bloom
6. **Ripening:** Once flowers and fruit reach full maturity, they'll need a couple of weeks of plain water devoid of nutrients. This process is called flushing as it allows the plants to use up all the nutrients they've previously absorbed

THE BEST METHODS FOR CARING FOR SEEDLINGS AFTER GERMINATION

Now's the time to put what you learned about the magic formula into action.

WATERING YOUR SPROUTS:

The basics for watering seedlings are like that of seeds. Only water your gems when the surface of the seed-starter mix feels dry. How fast your mix dries will depend on the temperature of the room and how much heat the light source provides. As your seedlings grow, I recommend sticking to the misting spray bottle to keep your little gems moist, but not too wet. Remember, they need oxygen to survive and over-watering can lead to drowning.

TO BOTTOM-WATER SEEDLINGS:

Find a pail large enough to hold your container and fill it with enough distilled or rainwater so that your container will sit in it. Place your container or cells into the pail of water and let it sit for 10 minutes. Check the moisture level of the soil by gently pressing your baby finger into the mix. If you push down to your knuckle and still don't feel moisture, keep the container in the water for up to 20 minutes more then remove any excess water. Bottom-watering provides great moisture for your seeds but it doesn't remove the salt or mineral deposits that form on the top layer of your soil, so I would suggest spraying the top of your soil every couple of weeks to rinse the soil and keep it fresh.

This is where I recommend using a fan to circulate the air and prevent disease. An area with good circulation also helps with reducing the chance of fungal spores, drying up the leaves after the soil's been sprayed and encourages the stems of your seedlings to grow more robust.

Pro Tip! If you don't have an oscillating or ceiling fan, do you have a forced-air furnace? Most thermostats for forced-air furnaces have an option to run the furnace fan continuously, which means the air in your home will always be circulating.

IDEAL TEMPERATURE FOR SEEDLINGS:

Your seedlings like to keep warm during the day and cool at night, just like they would if they were already in their outdoor environment. Try to keep your home between 70-90°F and if that's not possible, try using a supplemental heat source like a heat mat under your seedling tray. Turn off the mat for night and turn it back on in the morning. Temperatures above 90°F or below 70°F can lead to stunted root growth, so keep a close eye.

LET THERE BE LIGHT FOR SEEDLINGS:

Seedlings need a lot of light to keep them from getting weak and leggy. Try putting them in a sunny, south-facing window to expose them to as much light as possible during the day, but move them from windows at night to keep them away from cold drafts that stunt their growth. Make a habit of rotating your pots regularly. Your seedlings will naturally lean towards the light, but rotating them daily will straighten them back out. If you need to use artificial lighting, be sure to keep the lights just above the seedlings and raise the lights as they grow. Be sure to allow for 12-16 hours of light every day and remember that seedlings need darkness too.

THINNING TO THE HEALTHIEST PLANTS:

If you've sown multiple seeds per container and have more than one sprout per cell with their first set of true leaves, this is the time to thin your plants. I know, I wish we could keep them all too. I know they all look so lovely and innocent, but to thrive they need to be thinned. So how do you choose which ones to keep? Look for the strongest seedling in each cell. It will look the healthiest, have the thickest stem and be the most compact. Take a good look at them before cutting. The tallest ones don't always mean they're the healthiest ones. Tall could mean long and leggy, which happens when seedlings don't get enough light. If they're taller than the rest but look weak or flimsy, these are the ones you want to cut. If your seedlings all look uniformly similar, you can randomly choose which ones to remove or give it a bit more time to see if some of them get larger than the rest. But not too long. The longer you wait, the higher the risk of being overcrowded and having stunted growth. I wouldn't wait any longer than 3-4 sets of true leaves. If they all look relatively the same, there really isn't a right or wrong way of choosing at this point.

Be sure to use the right tools for thinning your seedlings. I have a pair of pink and grey handled bonsai shears that I love using. The blades are about 1.5" long, allowing me to get a close, precise cut every time. A micro-tip snip is an alternative to bonsai shears. Either way, be sure to disinfect the blades each time you use them. You can do this easily by dipping them into rubbing alcohol or by hand-washing them with soap and water.

When thinning your seedlings, you want to cut them off as close to the base as possible. NEVER pull the seedling from the soil. Pulling can lead to damaging and killing the roots of the plants that you're keeping. This is especially true for root crops (vegetables that grow underground). Damage done to the roots when plants were just seedlings often cause deformities that appear in plants later in life.

TRANSPLANTING YOUR SEEDLINGS TO LARGER CONTAINERS

Damping-off can be an enormous threat to seedlings. Just because they've already sprouted doesn't mean they're out of the dangerous woods. Contaminated containers or soil cause damping-off, which can make your little sprouts wither and possibly die. If you need to transplant your seedlings to larger containers before they're ready to head outside, make sure you wash and sterilize the containers thoroughly before transplanting. Wash with soapy water, rinse, and lightly spray them with peroxide and let dry.

FEEDING YOUR SEEDLINGS

One of the most basic seedling care tips to know is that seedlings don't require any supplemental fertilizer until the cotyledon is fully exposed and several sets of true leaves have grown. This makes seed-starter mixes so handy to use. When you use the 3 magic ingredients to make a great organic seed-starter mix, it will be full of all the essential nutrients your little gems will need until they get transplanted outside. Adding supplemental food too early can burn out tender roots and delicate foliage.

You should have **cotyledons** (first leaf or two) and groups of true leaves showing after the first few weeks of growing your seedlings. This means it's time to feed those little gems. By this point, they'll require regular feedings until it's time to transplant them outdoors into real soil or an enriched potting mix (**Chapter 9: Good Ol' Outdoors**). I make a fabulous organic fertilizer called Compost Tea, and it contains just 2 ingredients—**compost and water.** This stuff is cheap (free if you have your own compost) and works like liquid gold. Compost is full of nutrients that seedlings and future plants need. When it's soaked in water, those nutrients become liquid, making it easier to apply. Use it in a spray bottle to spray your leaves or use a watering can to apply directly to the base of your plants. Compost Tea works quickly by delivering its nutrients directly to the roots of your seedlings.

THE MAGIC POTION FOR COMPOST TEA

1. Fill a 5-gallon bucket ⅓ of the way with compost
2. Add distilled or rainwater up to 2" or so from the top of the bucket (Tap water is full of chlorine and should be avoided)
3. Stir it up to release the compost's nutrients into the water (think of it like dunking a tea bag and pressing on it with the back of a spoon)
4. Let the mixture sit for 5 days but continue stirring it a few times every day
5. On day 6, strain the compost mixture. Set the used compost

aside and keep the magic liquid. This is your ready-to-use Compost Tea!

It's ideal to apply your fertilizer in the mornings before the sun's rays get too intense. Water your seedlings with the tea every 5-7 days until it's time to transplant. After transplanting has been done, Compost Tea is safe to apply every 2 weeks or so.

POTTING ON

Potting on is easy to do, fun to say, and it takes time and patience. Whenever I use the term "potting on", I immediately think of Wayne's World when Wayne and Garth do their sing-song to "Party on! Excellent!!" Potting on! Excellent!! (I told you I'm an old school nerd. If you know what I'm referring to, good luck reading it any other way now).

In Case You Didn't Know: "Potting on" simply means transplanting seedlings into bigger containers than what they were originally planted in. This allows more space for their roots to grow and branch out into healthier, stronger, and more prominent seedlings.

When your little gems aren't so little anymore and it's still too cool to transplant them outdoors, you'll need to pot on those babies, maybe even twice. But this depends on what size of containers or cells you originally used, you may not need to do any potting on at all. Lucky you! That's never my case. As much as I put off doing this for as long as I can, I have little choice. If I use bigger containers for starting my seeds, I'd have to sacrifice how many seeds I sow because I'd lose precious space to needing larger containers. And I'd hate that a lot more than having to do the extra potting on work.

3 GOOD REASONS FOR POTTING ON

1. To avoid roots getting **root-bound.** Since a plant's health is directly related to its root health, being root-bound makes them a lot less likely to flourish. Potting on plants to larger containers means giving the roots room to grow without being restricted. When roots become squished, they grow around themselves in circles and can become a tangled mess. This affects how the roots thrive once the seedlings get transplanted to your outdoor garden. Plants with tangled roots can be gently loosened when transplanting, but this comes with risk. Some plants handle the ruffling up well while some can go through transplant shock from it. The best practice is to disrupt the roots as little as possible.

2. **As seedlings grow bigger, they drink more water and dry out faster.** When they're put into a larger environment, their soil will stay moist longer. Once you have some sprouts, you'll find that the starter-mix is drying out quicker than it did before germination occurred. Those little gems are thirsty!

3. **Potting on feeds the seedlings.** When seeds are sown in starter-mix, they'll be hungry once they run low on nutrients from the soil. Potting on means using more soil, which equals fresh nutrients.

There's no universal rule for when to pot on your seedlings. But you can time it based on container size, plant type, predicted time for being transplanted outside, and how quickly they're growing.

General Rule of a Green Thumb:
Container size matters. When a small seedling gets planted in too large a container, it could drown because the larger container holds more soil and water than what the seedling requires and the roots may struggle to establish themselves. Alternatively, seedlings could dry out being in too

large of a container as the water naturally gets drawn toward the edges of the container and away from the roots. The best practice is the "twice as large" rule. Transplant a 2" container to a 4" container, a 4" container to a 6" or 8" container, etc. Seedlings are fussy. They don't like being too cramped, but they do enjoy a light hug.

Use your original container size as a judgement for when you should start potting on. Small containers that have individual cells (usually a 6-pack) will need to be potted on sooner than the 3-4" wide individual ones. Plants started in 4" pots usually won't need to be potted on until they've reached 6-10 weeks old after germination (depending on the type of seedling). By this time, their roots will have reached the edges and bottom of the container, signaling that it's time to either pot on or transplant outside if the temperature is right. If it's too early to go outdoors, their next move would be to a 6" or 8" pot.

Pro Tip! Tomatoes are a larger plant, so prepare for them to outgrow their containers quickly. Many people plant tomatoes alongside peppers. I do it myself. They get sowed in the same size container, but the tomatoes will be ready for potting on much faster than the peppers.

In Case You Didn't Know: Terra-cotta pots are little thieves that absorb moisture. If you don't soak these pots before using them for planting, they will steal the water that you give your plants and can quickly lead to your seedlings drying out.

1. Choose a larger container by using the "twice as large" rule and make sure it has drainage holes so that your seedling won't be sitting in water.
2. Cover the drainage holes with a coffee filter to prevent the new soil from spilling out. The times where I didn't have a coffee filter on hand, I'd put a small, crumpled piece of paper into the hole to block the soil from falling out.
3. Give your seedling a good watering. This helps make the potting up process easier to adjust to and keeps the roots packed together.
4. Add a base layer of soil to the new container. This will act as a bed for the roots to rest on and grow into. Add enough soil so that your seedling should still be able to fit inside the container without running over the top.
5. Turn your seedling upside down, put your hand over the top of the container to provide a security net, and gently rotate the plant to coax it from its original container by letting it loosen and fall to your hand. Never just pull it out, you can damage the roots.
6. Place your seedling inside its new home. Try to center it as much as possible without burying the stem of small or tender seedlings (when the stem for these gets buried too deep, it could rot and kill the plant). Beans are an example. Otherwise, it's safe to plant most seedlings deeper and to surround the stem with soil. Tomatoes love being buried deep and can actually produce new roots from parts of the buried stem. If your seedlings have nice firm stems, it's usually safe to bury them a little deeper. Peppers, cabbage, broccoli, and kale don't mind going a little deeper either.
7. Press the seedling down gently but firm enough so that it settles in. Add more soil to cover it up, then give it a good watering. If you find the soil settled after watering, add more soil and water again.

That's all there is to it! You've potted on! Was that a wild ride, or what?!

General Rule of a Green Thumb:

If you notice your seedlings are just about ready for potting on but the outside temperature looks just about right for transplanting straight outdoors, I'd save the stress (for both you and your seedlings) and skip the indoor potting on practice and go straight outside. The only time you may reconsider this is if the roots are getting really balled up and cramped and you think it may stunt the plant's growth. If the roots are growing outside of its container, it's definitely time to pot on.

TIME TO HARDEN-OFF YOUR SEEDLINGS

Before taking your seedlings outside, like any good parent, you'll need to make sure they're ready for their new environment! They're so used to being tended to in their warm, cozy indoor greenhouse area that they don't know what it's like to be in the outside world. They need to go through a process called **hardening-off** before being exposed to all the outdoor elements.

Why do we need to do this? All seedlings have a wax coating (cuticle) that allows them to repel water, lowers dehydration rates, and filters UV rays. When seedlings grow indoors, they aren't able to fully develop their cuticle so they need time to build up their resistance to outdoor elements like wind, rain, direct sun, bugs, and various temperature changes. Preparing them to go outside will increase their chances of surviving the transplant process. This applies to vegetable, herb, and flower seedlings. Your little gems won't be happy if they're suddenly exposed to the outdoor elements for long periods, as this can lead to seedling disasters such as heat stress or transplant shock. Leaves can burn from the harsh sun, causing them to wilt, curl under, or even fall right off. Strong winds can weaken stems, causing some leggy ones to snap in half. Sudden cold temperatures can stop seedling growth or kill it altogether. (*How to Harden Off Plants for Transplanting*. 2021, April 7)

Hardening off is a simple process, but to do it right, it takes time and patience. But you're almost there! It's like preparing to send your kids off to school for the first time, you wouldn't do that without talking to them first about what they can expect to experience. No, I'm not saying hardening-off means having a discussion with your plants about what they can expect to find outside... well, you could—it wouldn't hurt! Exposing them to a little more carbon dioxide is never a bad thing. The hardening-off process takes several days, and it involves exposing your seedlings to the outdoors a little at a time. If you live in a region that has frost, plan to start your hardening-off schedule after the last predicted frost date.

General Rule of a Green Thumb:

The ideal nighttime temperature for hardening-off leafy greens or cool-weather seedlings (peas and beans) is when it reaches a consistent pattern of being in the low 50°Fs. Wait until the nighttime temperature reaches an average of being in the high 50°Fs for warm-weather plants like tomatoes, peppers, and squash.

HOW TO HARDEN-OFF YOUR SEEDLINGS IN ONE WEEK

When the outdoor temperature meets requirements and you have seedlings that are a couple of inches tall with at least one set of true leaves, start your hardening-off process indoors. Gently sweep your hand back and forth above the leaves of your seedlings to mimic a breeze. The air movement will strengthen the stems and prepare them for windy conditions. Do this for a few days.

Day 1

Find a spot outside when the temperature is above 60°F where there's partial sun and no wind. It's usually best to start this midafternoon. I have many shady trees in my yard that are perfect for this. Let your seedlings sit out there for 1-3 hours. Seedlings dry out quicker when outside, so be sure to check their moisture levels. After 3 hours max, bring your gems back inside.

Day 2

Put your seedlings outside in partial to full sun for a maximum of 3 hours, then bring them back inside. If it's a light windy day, that's OK. You're best to avoid strong winds though.

Day 3

Today, your seedlings should experience full sun for up to 4 hours with a soft breeze preferred. Check for moisture levels a couple of times and bring them back indoors after 3.5-4 hours.

Day 4

Take your seedlings outside in the morning today (when it's cooler out) and give them full sun for 5-6 hours. Make sure the soil stays moist and bring them back in after 6 hours max.

Day 5

It's a full day of sun for your seedlings today! Give them about 8 hours of full sun and breeze. If it's a hot day, they'll need to be watered at least twice so they don't dry out. Bring them inside at the end of the day.

Day 6

It's an exciting day! Your little gems are having their first sleepover tonight! As long as the temperatures stay well above freezing, that is. Put your seedlings outside in the morning, leave them out all day and overnight. Check for moisture levels throughout the day and evening and keep them off the ground for the night. The last thing you want is for them to become an all-night buffet for mice, rabbits, or other wild animals.

Day 7

You did it! You successfully hardened off your seedlings! It's now safe to transplant them to their permanent location! This is so exciting, I love this part!! I usually hope for a cloudy day 7 as sometimes plants don't do as well being transplanted in full sun. But by this stage, they usually pull through, having already been exposed to all the usual outdoor elements. Monitor the weather to make sure there's no frost predicted. If they're suddenly calling for frost and all your plants are already in containers or in the ground, protect them with a frost cover such as bedsheets, drop cloths, blankets, or plastic sheets. Stake them so they aren't touching the seedlings. Remove the coverings the next morning.

Well, you're getting closer to being a self-sufficient backyard homesteader! You can now make your own seed-starting mix using equal portions of the 3 magic ingredients—sphagnum peat moss, perlite, and vermiculite. You learned that rainwater is best for your plants (and it's free!) so don't forget to put your barrels out ASAP! And as far as needing pots for your seedlings, almost anything goes! It's great to repurpose things you would otherwise toss in the trash. You even learned how to make some cool DIY newspaper pots! And how about that super easy recipe for Compost Tea, eh? That's a quick, money-saving tip right there! You've learned how to care for your seeds and seedlings, and how to harden them off to the outside world. And when the timing is not yet right for transplanting outdoors, but your seedlings need more room to grow, I gave you the best method for potting on to a larger container.

I'd say these are almost enough fundamentals to take you through your beginner indoor seed garden! **In Chapter 9: Good Ol'**

Outdoors, I'm going to teach you all about the best techniques for transplanting your seedlings outdoors, and in **Chapter 10: I Beg Your Garden**, I'm going to talk about the basics of saving and storing seeds, so stay with me! Let's keep potting on as there are still some good thymes coming!!

Thank you for reading!

Enjoying so far?

Scan the QR code below
to leave a review!

THE
Garden
IS ♥ MY
happy
PLACE

9

GOOD OL' OUTDOORS

TRANSPLANTING

"When should I transplant my seedlings outside?"

"How tall should my seedlings be before I transplant them outside?"

"How do I transplant seeds to my outdoor garden?"

THESE ARE QUESTIONS I GET ASKED FREQUENTLY. AND LIKE everything else, there IS a right and wrong way to transplant your seedlings outdoors. Before you even consider moving your little gems to their permanent outdoor home, you need to be sure the temperature is in your seedlings' favor. There's no universal answer for this. Different seedlings need different conditions, so it's a good thing you kept all those seed packets! I plan around the last frost date, which can be tricky as it varies from year to year. Where I'm from there's usually no risk of frost by the end of May, middle of June, so I like to think it's safe to transplant around this time. Last year Mother Nature had other plans.

By May 20th, we had beautiful spring weather with daytime highs reaching 75°F and nighttime lows ranging between 55-60°F. I got all my seedlings transplanted, plus all the annual flowers that my neighbor had so generously gifted to me. She visited a local nursery and went spending crazy on all the gorgeous blooms they had. When she realized she bought too much for her garden, she asked me if I'd take some. Ummm...yes please! Anyway, things were growing exquisitely. All the seedlings had taken well to being transplanted, and I had just enough flowers to fill in my front rock garden. We had adequate rain in the evenings and beautiful, warm sunny days. Then June 15th hit. My mom called to say she heard there was a frost warning for that evening. Seriously?! It's June 15th. We had a daytime high of 70°F and I spent the afternoon suntanning on my deck. How could there be a frost warning?! I thought my mom was bonkers. There's no way we're getting frost that night. Sure enough, as the evening wore on, the temperature started dropping. Fast. I pulled out my phone and swiped over to the Weather Channel. Sure enough—frost warning.

I knew I should've listened to my mom. When will I ever learn moms are always right?! Especially my mom. There's no telling her any different, regardless of what the topic is about. Hi mom, if you're reading this—I, um, love you! I really do!

So. As the temperature dropped, I started scrambling for old bedsheets and drop cloths. Luckily, I found enough of them to spread over all my garden beds. (I have 5. 1 flower garden, 2 in-ground vegetable gardens, and 2 raised garden beds). But I didn't have enough to cover all my flower pots. (There's not a number for this, I had lots). So, it's already getting dark, I'm shivering in my shorts thinking that if I'm cold, I can imagine how chilly my seedlings must feel and it seems to get colder by the minute. I open my garage, shove some boxes into a corner and start moving my pots to the garage. 1...2...3...5...8...9...at least 12 pots later, my flowers are now safe from being frosted. What. a. pain. in. the......ugh. But oh, so worth it.

The next morning I went out early and there was a sheet of frost over everything! I waited for the sun to rise and took off all the sheets and drop cloths, praying that everything survived the night. I moved all my flower pots back outside and waited. Hours later, everything seemed to be OK! I checked the weather for that evening and again, frost warning. I ended up covering all the beds and moving all those pots for three nights in a row. Three nights of frost in the middle of June? This was highly unusual. But when transplanting your gems outside, it's something you need to plan for.

If you're prepared for "unexpected" foul weather, your plants will have a much higher survival rate. Situations like this are rare, but they happen. In most cases, you can't wait until the end of June to transplant your seedlings outside as you'll end up with a very short growing season. My best advice on what temperature to transplant your seedlings in would be to follow your local weather predictions and check a regional planting chart. You can find a ton of them online. When planning ahead, be sure the weather forecast doesn't call for any stormy or extreme weather such as frost, hail, high winds, or heavy rains for the next 6-8 days. You should also avoid transplanting on sweltering days, as this can lead to transplant shock. The best day is a calm, warm day. (Rhoades, H. 2020, September 14)

Did you know that there are over 24 types of outdoor gardens?!

- Vegetable gardens
- Flower gardens
- Herb gardens
- Raised garden beds
- Container gardens
- Vertical gardens
- Greenhouse gardens
- Tropical gardens
- Botanical gardens
- Succulent gardens
- Rock/zen gardens
- Deck/patio gardens

- Tire gardens
- And many more...

GETTING YOUR OUTDOOR SOIL READY

If you're transplanting your seedlings to an outdoor in-ground garden or a raised bed garden that was used previously, you'll need to make sure the soil is ready for fresh growth. Plants need many nutrients to grow tall and strong, and chances are your last year's crop drained much of this from the existing soil. The best additive for a small garden is a slow-release fertilizer combined with fresh soil. But if you're lucky enough to have that enormous garden I've always dreamed about with rows and rows of lush foliage, it's not economical to keep replacing the soil. For larger gardens, I recommend adding some aged compost to the soil and tilling it all up. And guess what? I have a recipe for that!

Bonus—this recipe can make your garden so well-composted that you can go a year or two without repeating the process!

MY ORGANIC, SLOW-RELEASE COMPOSTED GARDEN FERTILIZER

It takes a bit of time to prepare the ingredients for this fertilizer, so I'd suggest starting early. Its number one ingredient is.....kitchen scraps! Lots and lots of kitchen scraps. And almost anything goes. There are a few things you should definitely not include, but I'll list those separately.

Things you can and should include:

- Fruits and vegetables in any form—peels, scraps, raw or cooked, even rotting ones
- Nuts
- Eggshells

- Cooked foods such as rice, grains, bread, or eggs
- Paper products such as napkins, coffee filters, paper towels, or toilet paper rolls. Anything goes as long as it doesn't have a glossy coating on it (such as magazines)

Things you should avoid:

- Anything greasy
- Plastic, metal, or glass
- Dairy products such as cheese, milk, butter, or cream (these can attract unwanted pests and don't smell too nice when they decompose)
- Totally avoid meat—raw or cooked. Like dairy, they'll attract unwanted visitors to your garden and the smell of them decomposing is disgusting

If you have an organic lawn (free from weed-killers or other fertilizers), you can add grass clippings to your compost pile. Leaves are another great additive, and there's usually an abundance of those in the fall.

Once you decide on what you want to compost, put your items outside on a dry, level area or a compost bin if you have one, and sprinkle them with some wood ash or sawdust to help them decompose. Your compost bin should have a handle on it for ease of rotating the mix. The turning also adds oxygen to the mixture. Be sure your compost bin has some small holes in it to allow any excess moisture to leak out as you rotate the compost at least 2-3 times daily to get the best results.

Once your compost pile becomes a dark soil-like mixture, it's ready to be added to your gardens. Spread the mixture over your gardens using a pitchfork and watch for it to seep into the soil. That's all there is to it! Do this at least a week before you plan on transplanting your seedlings and then your soil will be ready to nurture its new inhabitants.

A self-sufficient backyard homesteader will always prefer doing things themselves with their own two hands, but if composting really isn't your thing, you can purchase a natural, slow-release fertilizer such as alfalfa meal, kelp meal or neem meal. These products come dry and need to be sprinkled on the soil and then watered. They'll each have specific instructions included on their packaging.

TIME TO PLAN OUT YOUR SEEDLINGS IN THE GARDEN

If you don't plan out enough space for your seedlings, it will become a competition for their survival. When they become crowded, they'll fight for nutrients, root and breathing space, and sunlight. Having to constantly fight makes them more prone to disease. Every seed packet should have its recommended spacing requirements for you to use as a guideline, but there are some general rules that you can follow:

- Thin your seedlings so that you're only sowing one plant per hole
- Most vegetables, herbs and flowers prefer as much sun as possible. But! There are many varieties that can do well in shaded areas and even prefer shade so again, check their packets before arranging their seating
- Space plants with large foliage such as broccoli, cauliflower, squash, and tomatoes at least 18-24" apart
- Plant smaller seedlings closer together, more like 12-18" depending on the type. Peppers, kale and leafy greens are all examples of smaller plants
- Direct-sow crops like carrots or radishes can grow closer together, usually only about an inch apart
- Don't worry about your garden looking sparse. This is only

111

temporary for allowing the seedlings adequate space to thrive. They will grow and your garden will fill in beautifully. Patience, young grasshoppaaah.

Pro Tip! You can alter the spacing requirements a bit by planting your seedlings in offset rows rather than in straight lines!

General Rule of a Green Thumb:

Plants like tomatoes, squash, corn, and peppers do best in full sun. They love the heat and can't get enough. But plants like leafy greens, cauliflower, peas, and green onions can tolerate some partial shade. Some nice plants that thrive and fill in your shaded areas are evergreen shrubs such as inkberry hollies and hemlocks, perennials such as jack-in-the-pulpits, leopard plants, and toad lilies, and annuals such as impatiens, wax begonias, and coleuses.

While our primary focus here is on starting seeds indoors and transplanting them outdoors, stay tuned for my next book; **"The Gardener's Guide to Organic Vegetable Gardening for Self-Sufficient Backyard Homesteaders"**, where I'll teach you the best practices for all things *outdoor gardening!* I'll go more in-depth about all the different **types of outdoor gardens, things to know, stuff you need, common mistakes and solutions, sowing, planting, transplanting, nurturing your garden, protecting your garden with your friends, foes, and the elements, reaping your rewards and so much more!** I am super excited to continue our garden journey together! But there is one last stop on this ride; **Saving your seeds!**

Stop
AND
Smell
THE
Flowers

10

SAVING SEEDS

& HARVESTING

SEED SAVING IS BECOMING QUITE THE SOCIAL MOVEMENT. IT WENT from being what dedicated gardeners would do to improve their gardens and preserve family heirlooms to friendly competitions amongst neighbors to see whose is biggest... *Snicker*. Nowadays, neighbors, friends, and relatives are all sharing seeds they've saved so they each can enjoy the best of the best. There are even various social media groups where seed-sharing has become popular. You too can get on the seed-saving train and start saving seeds with everything you'll learn throughout this chapter.

Why bother saving seeds, you ask? Besides the obvious reason for saving you some money by not having to buy new seeds, there's the satisfaction in being completely self-sufficient. You can regrow and relive some of your best-tasting vegetables and fruits or grow the same gorgeous flowers that were your favorites.

. . .

Choosing which seeds to save depends on many factors from the plant's life, from seed to yield. There are open-pollinated plants (also known as OP's) that are pollinated by wind, insects, or bees. If you're choosing an OP plant to save seeds from, you may need to take precautionary steps because cross-pollination can happen without you even knowing. This ends up creating a hybrid seed. Keeping different varieties of the same species far enough apart will lessen the possibility of creating a hybrid plant. But to be 100% sure that cross-pollination doesn't happen, cover the flowers of the selected plants with plastic bags until you can manually pollinate them (this is when you pollinate them by hand). Plants that are self-pollinating (autogamy) like tomatoes, beans, peas, eggplant, and peppers are great for beginner seed savers. Tomatoes aren't the easiest to play with for seed extraction, but I'll share my best method for doing this later on in the chapter. If you're saving flower seeds, you can start with snapdragons, marigolds, and zinnias. These flowers are also self-pollinating. They're often referred to as "complete" or "perfect" because they don't need anyone but themselves to pollinate. All it takes is a little wind action and they're good to go! As long as pollen passes from the stamen (male reproductive part) to the pistil (female reproductive part), pollination will occur. (*Modern Farmer.* (2018, *October 19*)

In Case You Didn't Know: Autogamy *means being able to self-pollinate. This happens when a flower has both the male and female parts needed for self-pollination.*

Selecting the best seeds to save also depends on local weather trends and your individual tastes or preferences. Some qualities and traits worth considering when choosing seeds to save are:

- No disease or insect issues throughout its life
- Does not bolt early
- Thrives in conditions specific to your area (hot, warm, cool, etc.)

- Size (do you prefer bigger or smaller plants)
- Early blooming
- Best tasting
- Most juicy
- The highest yield per plant
- Early to produce
- Perfect or unique coloring
- Extended blooming season
- Desirable fragrance
- Strong and robust
- Vegetable shelf life

THERE ARE 3 PLANT CATEGORIES YOU CAN COLLECT
SEEDS FROM: ANNUALS, PERENNIALS, AND BIENNIALS.

ANNUALS

Annual vegetable plants and flowers produce seeds the same year as they're sowed and need to be replanted yearly. Examples of annuals are tomatoes, peppers, peas, green and yellow beans, lettuce, onions, squash, pumpkins, eggplant, soybeans, melons, broccoli, dusty millers, petunias, marigolds, coleus, pansies, and celosias.

PERENNIALS

Perennial plants don't require replanting each year as they produce seeds once they reach a certain age. That age differs for each species. Some popular examples of perennials are asparagus, chives, Caucasian spinach, Chinese yams, leaf celery, rhubarb, roses, peonies, black-eyed Susans, chrysanthemums, lilies, and tulips.

BIENNIALS

Biennial plants are mainly root vegetables with a few exceptions like kale and parsley. **Biennials produce their crop during the first year they're sowed but won't produce seeds until the following year.** It takes 2 years to complete their life cycle. Biennial flowers will produce their leaves the first year, but the actual flowers won't bloom until the second year. Kale, carrots, turnips, celery, cabbage, parsley, parsnips, brussels sprouts, hollyhocks, canterbury bells, foxgloves, sweet Williams, and forget-me-nots are all good examples of biennial plants.

Most beginner seed savers will start with **annual seeds**, as they're the easiest to play with. Once you've examined all your plants from seedlings to crop or flower production, select the qualities and traits important to you and flag those particular plants. I use plant stakes, ribbon, or chicken wire to mark the plants I want to keep as future seed-bearing plants. You can use anything that will make the plant stand out so that the specific fruit or vegetable doesn't get harvested on you. The crop needs to ripen on the plant for the seeds to mature and be viable for saving. Take extra precautions to stop birds and animals from munching on your seed source. But don't favor that plant over any other either. You want to treat the seed source plant the same as you treat the others so that it stays true to its nature. Coddling and being overprotective will not produce a naturally strong seed. (*Seed Savers Exchange. 2021, January 1*)

THERE ARE 3 DIFFERENT SEED CATEGORIES:

1. **Plants that shatter** (brassicas, onions, and lettuce plants) all release their seeds upon ripening. If you're wanting to save seeds from this category, tie a cloth bag around the developing seeds, so they don't automatically get released into the wind. Most flowers fall under this category.

2. **Edible seeds** such as peas, corn, and beans should stay on the plant until they have dried. This process is called curing and is the time it takes for a seed to dry out enough to be stored. After collecting edible seeds and removing the dried pods and husks, you'll need to let the seed continue to cure so that it loses all its moisture.

3. **Fleshy fruits and vegetables** such as tomatoes, cucumbers, zucchini, melons, peppers, and so many others, have seeds that sit right in the edible flesh. Leave these crops to slightly over-ripen before harvesting for the seeds. Tomatoes should soften, the peppers should show signs of aging such as wrinkles, and the cucumbers should turn yellow, which is a sign that their seeds are ready. You basically need to leave these guys past the point of eating them. If they're too ripe to eat, the seeds are ready for harvest. But don't let them rot—the heat of the decomposing flesh may make the seeds non-viable. Once you have harvested the seeds, the flesh should never dry on the seed. Start the flesh removing process as soon as possible. I'll explain how to do this shortly.

CLEANING AND DRYING YOUR SEEDS

After you've collected your seeds, you'll need to clean and dry them further. The seeds from plants that shatter are most painless because all you have are seeds—no debris or pods to separate. Lay them out on newspaper to dry for at least a week. If the seeds are wet, the newspaper will need to be changed periodically to ensure a nice, dry condition. If you don't have the room to do this properly, then an alternate method is using equal parts silica gel or powdered milk to seeds. You don't want to mix the seeds with the gel or milk, so put one or both in cloth bags and seal them in an airtight container. (They can be in the same container, they just can't mix)

- Leave small seeds sealed for 8-12 days

- Leave large seeds sealed for 12-16 days

Edible seeds like beans and peas will need their pods removed. By now, they're very dry and brittle, so they should break away easily. If you don't have many seed pods to remove, then you may as well do them by hand and you'll skip the tedious step of having to separate the seeds from the debris. When you have more than what you can do by hand (which is usually more than a handful), you'll need to "thresh" them.

In Case You Didn't Know: Threshing *is the term used to remove the seeds from the seed heads. The seed head is whatever holds the seed. In peas or beans, it would be the pod. For corn, it would be the cob. You can purchase a tool specifically for threshing called a flail. It looks similar to a nunchuck where it has a long wooden handle that swivels a second piece of wood that smacks the seed heads.*

Fun Fact! Have fun while threshing! Skip the flail and just slap handfuls of seed heads against a hard, clean surface like the inside of a sterile bucket or trash can (which hopefully catches most of your flying seeds). Or you can use clean sheets to lay your seed heads on and cover them up with another clean sheet, then walk (or put on some tunes and dance) right on top of them. Both methods will separate the seeds from the seed heads, but then you'll need to pick through the debris to find the seeds. The energy you let out in doing this makes the sifting so worth it.

Screening, exactly as it sounds, is another method for cleaning seeds. Sieve the seeds through the screen and toss away the larger debris. Then select a screen size that will hold the seeds and allow the smaller debris to fall through. Pieces of unwanted debris will remain, but this is where winnowing comes into play.

In Case You Didn't Know: Winnowing is when you dump the contents from one container into another outside in a pleasant breeze or by using the air from a gentle fan. This takes a bit of practice, so lay a sheet down in case your seeds miss the target (your second container). This will eliminate the lighter debris, leaving just your seeds. This method is often used with flower seeds since they're usually pretty tiny. Their size makes it harder to separate them from their debris. Make sure it's not too windy, or your seeds will take off on you too!

The seeds from the fleshy fruits and vegetables are by far the most time-consuming. The flesh needs to be removed entirely. The best way to do this is to put the seeds in a pot or bowl of water and let them sit for a few days. The pulp will rise to the top and the seeds will sink to the bottom. Dump out the floating flesh and repeat until your seeds are completely naked of flesh. Remove the seeds from the water and set them out to dry on newspaper. Again—replace the wet newspaper when needed.

Pro Tip! If seeds dry too quickly, they may shrink or crack. This makes using an oven or auxiliary heat source pretty risky. If you want the best results, stick to the manual method.

Once you have your seeds dried, it's time to store them. You can use any tight-sealing jar, can, or container. Make sure it seals tight—your seeds will absorb any humidity they can, which will reduce their viability when it comes time for germination. Put your seeds in envelopes and don't forget to label them with their name and date collected. I use mason jars. I like how they seal and am comfortable that they won't let in any moisture. Where do you store them? Scientists did all the hard work for us and have discovered that the best temperature to store seeds at is between 32°-41°F. This makes your fridge the ideal place to keep them safe. If you can't spare the space inside your refrigerator, then find a cool, dark spot inside your home as the second-best place to store them. (Modern Farmer. (2018, October 19)

SEED VIABILITY

Viability means having the ability to germinate. If you've made good choices in which seeds to save and you've followed the ripening and drying procedures, then there should be good reason to expect your seeds to be viable. Age is always a factor. Seeds should be viable for 2-3 years or even longer. You can do your own little scientific test if you ever question whether the seeds you saved are viable. Or if you have bought seeds but aren't sure exactly how old they are.

Take some of your seed stash and place them on a wet paper towel. Roll it up and put it in a plastic ziplock bag. Label and store it in a warm place between 70-80°F. Check on the seeds in a few days to see if germination has occurred. You should already know the timeframe for germination since you wrote it on your label, right? If after that time only some seeds germinate, then leave them for 1 week past their regular germination time frame. Count how many germinated from your total to get the rate of germination. Example: If 8/10 seeds germinated, then you have an 80% viability rate. Smart, eh?

SEED-SAVING TIPS FOR 3 DIFFERENT PLANT TYPES

Pumpkins and Squash

If you choose to save seeds from pumpkins or squash, then pay attention! Make sure your seed choice, pumpkin or squash, is of pure nature. This means they're not crossbred with another pumpkin or squash variety. Pumpkins and squash will never mix with each other, but there are many varieties of each that might crossbreed amongst themselves.

There are male and female blossoms on each plant. The female is easy to spot by the bulge on her stem underneath the flower. The bulge makes it look like she is pregnant. The male flower has just a straight, skinny stem, so there should be no problem telling them apart. You'll have way more male blossoms compared to female blossoms. In fact, you might see only male blossoms for the first couple of weeks, wondering where on earth did all the girls go?!

Female blossoms on pumpkin and squash open early in the morning and close back up shortly after. You can tell when a female has opened and then closed by her slightly droopy, wrinkled look.

When you find a female bud, you'll want to tag the vine with a ribbon so you don't lose where she is. The vines grow real fast and can throw you off from where she's hiding.

Since you've been keeping a daily eye, you'll know what the blossom looks like when it's ready to bloom. Once your seed choice blossom looks ready to bloom, tape the petals so it can't open and allow in any early morning bees or wasps. Also, find an unopened male on the same vine or from the same variety and tape the petals so it can't open either. Remove the tape from both flowers the following day. Take the male flower off the vine and peel off its petals to expose its stamen (male part). Gently open the petals of the female so you can hand pollinate it by rubbing the pollen from the male directly onto the pistil (female part). Tape up the female again so no bees or wasps can get in. The petals will usually fall off within a day or two, so no worries about cross-pollination after that.

Mark your seed source pumpkin or squash with a bright ribbon so you'll know which one it is when it comes time to harvest.

Dill

Dill is a herb essential in the pickling process. If you decide to grow pickling cukes, then growing your own dill to pair it with is an absolute delight. It's so easy to save seeds from dill. Cut the seed heads off (don't just pull them or you'll lose a lot of seeds) and store them indoors in a paper bag for a few weeks. After the drying period, rub the seed heads with both hands and the seeds will fall right off. Put them in a labeled envelope and into your seed jar.

Leaf Lettuce

This self-pollinating salad green is another easy seed-saving breed. Choose the plant that bolted last. The flowers will turn into seed heads. Put a cloth bag around the seed head if you want to keep all the seeds. If you want to keep just a couple dozen seeds, then shake the bolted stalk and catch the seeds with a bowl or pail. You'll have to winnow the fluff and debris away and then let the seeds completely dry out for a week. Now they're ready for storage.

SEED BANKS

Wars, natural disasters, and changing climate conditions continue to disrupt the efforts of saving our seed heritage. All countries have different wild varieties of the many crops we steadily rely on—grains, fruits, vegetables, and flowers. Trying to get all countries on board with protecting and saving wild seeds is a task. The Crop Trust Global Seed Vault in Norway has been fighting this seed war since 2008. It has amassed over 1 million different varieties of seeds from almost every country in the world. The Vault has the capability of holding 4.5 million different varieties of seeds, equaling a maximum of 2.5 billion seeds. The existence of this Global Seed Vault doesn't exempt us from doing our part in staying true to our heritage by continuing to grow the Heirloom varieties of fruits, vegetables, and flowers that were passed down from generation to generation.

To be considered an Heirloom seed, a seed needs to be grown in a specific area for a minimum of 50 years. But many Heirlooms have been growing for centuries. The fruits and vegetables grown from some of these plants will be exactly what your grandmother's, grandmother's, grandma grew. These Heirlooms might not have been the best yielding, have the perfect color, or maybe didn't travel to their destinations well—but because they've been growing in the same local conditions for generations, they've built up certain resistant traits to at least produce a reliable, edible crop.

GMO seeds (Genetically Modified Organisms), or scientifically engineered seeds, are seeds that have taken over most of the world's crops. These seeds are susceptible to total extinction because they are too genetically similar to each other. If a disease or insect was to attack a specific GMO crop, then it, and any varieties of it, could be wiped right off the planet.

Well, those are the basics of how to harvest and save seeds from your favorite flowers and vegetables. Enjoy them again next year or show off your new gardening skills and share them with friends and family as you brag about how good you're getting at backyard homesteading! Heirloom seeds are our sustainable future and the future of our children's children. So to all you seed-savers (or should I say you seed-saving heroes) of the world, keep doing what you're doing. Try your best to make sure the seeds you save are exactly what you claim them to be. This means you must take steps to protect the Heirloom varieties and ensure no cross breeding occurs.

MY GARDEN CALENDAR

SCAN ME

Use this **tool & spreadsheet** to discover **your zone** and the **best time of year to sow, plant and harvest your fruits & veggies!**

go to:

WWW.BACKYARDHOMESTEADCOMMUNITY.COM

CONCLUSION

This is it! You made it to the end! With my rock *salad* foundation, you're now well on your way to becoming a more self-sufficient backyard homesteader!

You started on this journey by learning what a seed needs to thrive—water, oxygen, light, and temperature. I covered some of the easiest seeds to start indoors and ones that you may want to avoid (at least for a few seasons until you have all the basics down pat). I revealed the 3 magic ingredients in my homemade seed-starter mix—sphagnum peat moss (or its alternative), perlite, and vermiculite. The outstanding qualities in this formula will give your seeds the best chance at success: water retention, soil aeration, and even distribution of nutrients.

There are so many types of equipment available to make your indoor seed-starting experience easier and more successful:

- Entire seed-starting systems complete with lights and humidity domes
- Humidifiers to keep your growing area humid
- Heating mats to help heat the soil for germination

- Many auxiliary lighting options
- Timers to operate lights
- Fans to circulate the air and help your seeds prepare for outdoor conditions.

I gave you fair warning about the 12 most common mistakes made by beginner seed-starters so you can better prepare yourself for success:

1. Not enough light
2. Too little or too much water
3. Starting too early in the season
4. Sowing too deep
5. Transplanting outdoors too soon
6. Sowing too many seeds
7. Soil too cool
8. Not labeling
9. Giving up too soon
10. Using old or stale seeds
11. Not using proper seed-starter mix
12. Not reading the seed packet

You'll have a significant head start if you can avoid these mistakes!

I went through the importance of using sterile ingredients in your seed-starter mix and a few methods of sterilizing your mix if needed. You learned the major differences between starter-mix and potting soil and the importance of wetting your mix before you fill your pots and sow your seeds. This prevents you from needing to add mix when it all settles, which throws off your perfectly planned depths. I talked about bottom-watering and capillary mats and how not to take shortcuts with cheap felt when it comes time to replace the mat.

I gave you my entire step-by-step process of how to sow seeds successfully indoors. From filling your containers with mix, choosing the best seeds to plant, sowing at the right depth, sowing 2 seeds per pot, the importance of the initial watering and labeling, and the correct use of humidity domes and heat mats. I walked you through the 5 stages of a seed's life and how they need warmth, light (or no light), and water to germinate. Some seeds need help to thin their coat so they can better absorb water and some need temperature shocking to wake them from dormancy. You learned about the 6 stages of a plant's life:

1. Sprout
2. Seedling
3. Vegetative
4. Budding
5. Flowering
6. Ripening

I discussed thinning the seedlings to keep only the healthiest and how to pot on to bigger containers when the seedling has outgrown its original pot but is too cold outside to be planted outdoors. I gave you my special recipe for compost tea so you can feed your seedlings all the nutrients they need.

You discovered seedlings shouldn't be transplanted outside without being hardened-off first, and how using my step-by-step hardening-off guide will walk you through getting them ready for the great outdoors! Plot out where you'll be transplanting your seedlings by using the instructions on the packet. Check for spacing and sun/shade conditions. Always check your local weather report to make sure there isn't any extreme weather on the way before committing to your transplant date. Tilling the soil and adding some compost or slow-release fertilizer will get your soil ready for its new tenants. You have a detailed list of what you can and can't put in your homemade compost.

Savings seeds is important for our future and is a great money-saving idea. You learned how to keep a seed source plant from cross-breeding and some tricks for keeping some specific seed varieties like pumpkins or squash, dill, and leaf lettuce. You also now know the difference between annuals, perennials, and biennials and how to collect and clean the seeds through threshing, screening, and winnowing. What did you think about my neat trick on how to clean fleshy fruits and vegetables like tomatoes and pumpkins? Our ancestors saved seeds for generations, keeping some of the Heirloom plants and flowers alive and still in existence today. Scientists have "perfected" some of the seed crops by genetically engineering them for specific things like size, color, growing better in cold/warm climates, etc. But what they've ultimately done is make so many crops around the world so genetically similar that they could easily be wiped out in one season from potential disease and insect problems. Individual gardeners like you and I should continue saving seeds so that our future generations will have seeds to grow, even if the world is hit with a seed pandemic that ruins some of their existence.

I'm sad that our seed-starting adventure has come to an end, but I am ecstatic to say that our journey together is far from over! You've done all the indoor work—your little gems are hardened off and getting transplanted outside! But what about your outdoor garden? There's so much more to learn, so I hope you'll continue learning with me throughout my next book, **"The Gardener's Guide to Organic Vegetable Gardening for Self-Sufficient Backyard Homesteaders"**.

You have all the tools and resources you need, get out there and kick some *asparagass!!*

"The detail and information given is beyond what I ever expected. So many questions I never asked or thought about were answered. I don't understand how the author could possibly cover everything, but yes, answers are there for any question you have."

- Verified Purchaser

"This was a little gem of a gardening book. I found it to be well formatted, easy to read, well organized, and it provided a ton of information on seed starting."

- Verified Purchaser

"I enjoyed reading this book. I learned more about starting seeds indoors. I wish I had this book at the beginning of the year. I did have some successful seeds that germinated, grew to seedlings and got transplanted into my outdoor garden. There are some helpful tips that I will try next season."

- Verified Purchaser

"it is good, clear, has short sentences, and avoids being convoluted."

- Verified Purchaser

Thank you for reading!
Did you enjoy this book?
Scan the QR code below to leave a review!

BIBLIOGRAPHY

Back To Reality. (2017, March 7). *How We Set Up Our Germination Station for Starting Seedlings Indoors.* YouTube. https://www.youtube.com/watch?v=Kn0IdclkDYw

Bio Advanced. (2021, January 1). *The Basics Of Saving Seeds | Bioadvanced.* https://www.bioadvanced.com/articles/basics-saving-seeds

Britannica. (2021). *photosynthesis.* Britannica Kids. https://kids.britannica.com/kids/article/photosynthesis/353624

C. Boeckmann (2021, January 6). *Starting Seeds Indoors: How and When to Start Seeds.* Old Farmer's Almanac. https://www.almanac.com/starting-seeds-indoors-how-and-when-start-seeds

Epic Gardening. (2019, March 3). *Seed Starting Indoors Under Grow Lights 101.* YouTube. https://www.youtube.com/watch?v=txmGMePY9OU

Epic Gardening. (2021, February 15). *My NEW Favorite Seed Starting Method.* YouTube. https://www.youtube.com/watch?v=zX3eePK5ifU

Epic Gardening. (2020, January 28). *Answering 18 of Your Seed Starting Questions!* YouTube. https://www.youtube.com/watch?v=puKe3WbAbPk

G. (2018, March 9). *Germinating Seeds Indoors & Caring for Seedlings*. Age Old. https://www.ageold.com/germinating-seeds-indoors-caring-for-seedlings/#:%7E:text=Remember%2C%20most%20seeds%20will%20germinate,speed%20up%20the%20germination%20process.

Gardeners.com. (2021, January 28). *Prevent Seedling Disease With a Fan, Damping-Off: Gardener's Supply*. https://www.gardeners.com/how-to/fan-seedlings/8612.html

Gardener's Supply Company. (2021, May 4). *How to Start Seeds - Germinating Seeds | Gardener's Supply*. Gardeners.Com. https://www.gardeners.com/how-to/how-to-start-seeds/5062.html#:%7E:text=Choose%20potting%20soil%20that%27s%20made,to%20moisten%20the%20planting%20mix.

Gary Heilig, Michigan State University Extension. (2021, March 9). *Potting soils and seed-starting mixes for your garden*. MSU Extension. https://www.canr.msu.edu/news/potting_soils_and_seed_starting_mixes_for_your_garden

Grows, M. (2018, May 4). *The Importance of Being Labeled*. Maryland Grows. https://marylandgrows.umd.edu/2018/05/04/the-importance-of-being-labeled/

Hemingway, M. (2019, January 30). *Best Seed Starting Mixes: Reviews & Recommendations*. Gardening Products Review. https://gardeningproductsreview.com/best-seed-starting-mixes/

Ianotti, M. (2021, April 7). *How to Harden Off Plants for Transplanting*. The Spruce. https://www.thespruce.com/how-to-harden-off-plants-1402554

JoegardenerTV. (2019, February 20). *How I Start Seeds Indoors Tips & Techniques*. YouTube. https://www.youtube.com/watch?v=5ypS6tT8vlk

John Vanzile, J. V. (2020, July 29). *Increase Your Home's Humidity to Help Houseplants Thrive*. The Spruce. https://www.thespruce.com/increase-humidity-for-houseplants-1902801

K State. (2020, March 2). *Lighting options for starting seed (LEDs vs. Fluorescent)*. https://www.johnson.k-state.edu/lawn-garden/agent-articles/vegetables/lighting_options_for_Seeds.html

Kring, L. (2021, March 22). *13 of the Best Grow Lights for Indoor Plants and Seedlings*. Gardener's Path. https://gardenerspath.com/gear/best-grow-lights/

Ly, L. (2021, February 6). *Make the Best Seed Starting Mix for Dirt Cheap (It's Organic Too)*. Garden Betty. https://www.gardenbetty.com/how-to-make-your-own-seed-starting-and-potting-mix/

Michaels, K. (2021, December 2). *Don't Make These Common Seed Starting Mistakes*. The Spruce. https://www.thespruce.com/growing-seeds-indoors-common-mistakes-847800

MIgardener. (2021, February 18). *8 Most Common Seed Starting Mistakes (FINALLY Starting Seeds)*. YouTube. https://www.youtube.com/watch?v=aJHiYC-Im9Y

MIgardener. (2021b, February 18). *8 Most Common Seed Starting Mistakes (FINALLY Starting Seeds)*. YouTube. https://www.youtube.com/watch?v=aJHiYC-Im9Y

Modern Farmer. (2018, October 19). *Seed Saving 101: 10 Things to Know If You Want to Start Saving Seeds*. https://modernfarmer.com/2018/07/seed-saving-101-10-things-to-know-if-you-want-to-start-saving-seeds/

Myefe. (2020, December 1). *SW7 Single*. https://myefe.com/transcription-pronunciation/nasturtium#:%7E:text=Transcription%20and%20pronunciation%20of%20the,in%20British%20and%20American%20-variants.&text=a%20South%20American%20trailing%20plant,widely%20grown%20as%20an%20or-namental.

O'Donnell, J. (2020, April 7). *How to Water Seeds and Seedlings*. Gardening Channel. https://www.gardeningchannel.com/how-to-water-seeds-and-seedlings/

Rhoades, H. (2020, September 14). *StackPath*. Gardening Know How. https://www.gardeningknowhow.com/garden-how-to/propagation/seeds/when-to-transplant-a-seedling-plant-into-the-garden.htm

Roy, B. (2018, November 4). *The Importance of Humidifiers in a Grow Room Setup*. Pure Natural Systems. https://blog.purennatural.com/the-importance-of-humidifiers-in-a-grow-room-setup

S. (2020, May 14). *The Best Timer for Grow Lights - 6 Top Choices*. Best LED Grow Lights Info. https://bestledgrowlightsinfo.com/the-best-timer-for-grow-lights-6-top-choices/

Seed Savers Exchange. (2021, January 1). *How to Save Seeds - Seed Savers Exchange*. https://www.seedsavers.org/how-to-save-seeds

Wikipedia contributors. (2020, December 7). *Photomorphogenesis*. Wikipedia. https://en.wikipedia.org/wiki/Photomorphogenesis#:)

Wikipedia contributors. (2021, March 7). *Cotyledon*. Wikipedia. https://en.wikipedia.org/wiki/Cotyledon

Printed in the USA
CPSIA information can be obtained
at www.ICGtesting.com
LVHW050751240124
769293LV00003B/104